MW01468959

TOTAL SATURATION IN THE Spirit-Empowered LIFE

VOL 1: GOD'S EMPOWERING PRESENCE IN US

WENDY J. CLARK

Cover design by Wendy J. Clark

ISBN: 978-1-7354954-9-1

All scripture references from NKJV unless otherwise quoted. All Greek and
Hebrew definitions used in whole or in part from Strong's Concordance.
Other references as follows:
† Helps Word-Studies
‡ Berean Strong's Lexicon
* Thayer's Greek Lexicon
§ Brown-Driver-Briggs

Thanks to Biblehub.com for providing such great
Online tools to study the Word of God

SWORD OF THE SPIRIT & POWER OF THE TONGUE
SPEAK IT®

Thank you, Lord. Life in Christ is so much more than I could've ever asked or imagined...

> Now to Him who is able to do exceedingly abundantly above all that we ask or think, according to the power that works in us,
> **EPHESIANS 3:20**

To those who are still trying to do it themselves...

> I have been crucified with Christ; it is no longer I who live, but Christ lives in me; and the life which I now live in the flesh I live by faith in the Son of God, who loved me and gave Himself for me.
> **GALATIANS 2:20**

To those who believe...

> that the God of our Lord Jesus Christ, the Father of glory, may give to you the spirit of wisdom and revelation in the knowledge of Him, the eyes of your understanding being enlightened; that you may know what is the hope of His calling, what are the riches of the glory of His inheritance in the saints, and what is the exceeding greatness of His power toward us who believe, according to the working of His mighty power
> **EPHESIANS 1:17-19**

CONTENTS

ENDORSEMENTS

Wendy J. Clark's most recent work, *Total Saturation in the Spirit-Empowered Life,* is a very helpful and thrilling resource. We have enjoyed each of Wendy's books, and have used them in our personal devotional time but also in larger Bible study settings as well. We would encourage any believer who desires to grow and be further established in the redemptive work of Jesus to read time and again, and let these truths saturate your soul! You will find great personal edification as well as the work of the Spirit manifesting mightily in your midst.

Keith & Heidi Hershey
FOUNDERS: MUTUAL FAITH MINISTRIES INTL.

As long as I have known her, Wendy has been a voracious student and teacher of God's Word. Her longing to see His Truth manifest, not only in her own life, but the lives of everyone around her, has been the motivation for her labor of love. This is not a quick or light read, but an iron-sharpening-iron tool to explore and discover the revelation necessary to experience the fullness of living in and by the Holy Spirit, as God has provided for all believers. Why settle for a trickle when we can have *Total Saturation in the Spirit-Empowered Life?*

Debra Arnott
DEAN OF KINGDOM MOVEMENT SCHOOL OF MINISTRY

Wendy J. Clark has done it again! Her first two books, *30 Days Saturation in Healing* and *The Finished Work of Christ* have truly been transformational for many in our groups. Lives are being changed and faith is arising. Praise God!

Wendy uses Scripture throughout, and simple, easy to understand language to tackle deep Biblical subjects. She is a great expositor of the Word of God, digging into the original languages and teaching us to do the same. Her explanations address many of the lies the enemy tries to get us to believe. Through these practical teachings, we can embrace the full truth of God's Word and apply our faith to it.

Now with the release of *Total Saturation in the Spirit-Empowered Life,* Wendy has provided churches, small groups and individuals with an invaluable tool to deepen their understanding of what it means to *"walk in the Spirit and not in the flesh."* With powerful study tools to better understand the Greek and Hebrew, and now with the addition of *Living Word Concepts,* the student can go even deeper into understanding what the intent of the Holy Spirit was when He inspired the writers to pen the pages of the Word of God. All laced with the unconditional, everlasting love of God that brings believers into great security and peace.

Well done Wendy! You and your labor of love are a tremendous blessing to the body of Christ and it is safe to say that *"for such a time as this"* you were born.

Keith & Victoria A. Winterowd
CO-PASTORS: MONKEYPOD TREE MINISTRIES

Ephesians 6:12 (NIV) says, *"For our struggle is not against flesh and blood, but against the rulers, against the authorities, against the powers of this dark world and against the spiritual forces of evil in the heavenly realms."* Wendy's detailed research and scriptural insights give you wisdom on accessing the power of the Holy Spirit in your life.

Kathleen Cooke
CO-FOUNDER: COOKE MEDIA GROUP & THE INFLUENCE LAB/INFLUENCE WOMEN
AUTHOR: HOPE 4 TODAY: STAY CONNECTED TO GOD IN A DISTRACTED CULTURE

Words create pictures, pictures create understanding, understanding becomes our reality.

Wendy J. Clark has a God-given gift of taking challenging concepts in the Word and making them simple. Her word pictures are theological commentary, driving the point home and eliminating the use of a thousand words. Through every topic, regardless of complexity, she won't take you to the edge of a thought or revelation and leave you hanging. She'll complete the idea and place a revelatory picture in your mind, making it easy to embrace and share with others.

Morris Adams
SENIOR PASTOR: LIVING IN THE WORD CHURCH

LIVING WORD CONCEPTS EXPLAINED

FOLLOWING THE NUMBER TRAIL

As in previous Speak It® books, there are important superscript numbers in the text. These are not footnotes but essential for connecting the text of the book to referencing scriptures and Greek and Hebrew word definitions.

But now, this numerical system has been expanded and globalized into a powerful new tool called *Living Word Concepts.*

Just like in previous books, when you see "How do we *walk*[12] in the *Spirit-empowered life?*"[3] these numbers point to the same number in a scripture box, and sometimes to a key Greek or Hebrew word on the page and throughout the chapter.

Globalization of this numerical system means that the number for *walk*[12] will always be number 12. The number for the *Spirit-empowered life,*[3] or related words and concepts like the *power of God,*[3] the *resurrection power,*[3] and the *Holy Spirit,*[3] will always be number 3. The global index of these words and concepts that have been grouped together are found in the *Living Word Concepts* in the back of the book.

THREE WAYS TO USE LIVING WORD CONCEPTS

1/ When you see a superscript number, look out for that same number and connect to other occurrences on the page and throughout the chapter. It's your job to make the connections yourself between the text of the book and the accompanying scriptures and word definitions. Take the time to read each scripture and each definition. In doing so, associated thoughts will be made apparent, and deeper meanings that solidify your understanding will become clear. So keep your eyes open and follow the numeric trail.

2/ Look up the corresponding number in the *Living Word Concepts* at the back of the book and read the words and concepts that are grouped together under the same number. Meditate on these connections and consider how they are related to each other. Your scriptural understanding will rapidly expand in ways you may never have considered.

3/ Take the time to study the *Living Word Concepts* by themselves. Consider each numbered group and let the scriptural understanding expand your overall Biblical revelation.

Living Word Concepts is an ever-expanding resource that will be continually updated. Check **SpeakItPower.com/LivingWordConcepts** to see the most current version.

Total Saturation in the Spirit-Empowered Life is so dense with Biblical revelation that it's crucial you read it slowly. Take the time to chew each mouthful until you receive every ounce of nutrition. Don't read more than one chapter at a time. Read each chapter multiple times. Read each scripture and word definition. Follow the numerical trail. Most importantly, pray in tongues and ask God to reveal things to you that you have never seen before (Jer 33:3).

> Call to Me, and I will answer you, and show you great and mighty things, which you do not know.' **JER 33:3**

STUDY FOCUS POINTS

Wherever you see the following graphic bullets pause and reflect. They highlight some important points to take special note of.

FOUNDATIONAL FOOTPRINT

This is a fundamental doctrinal truth that needs to be clearly understood to have correct foundational knowledge of Scripture.

SATURATION POINT

Meditate on this until it drops into your spirit as a revelation. Don't be quick to move on from here—really focus and soak this one in.

❶ THE LAW OF FIRST MENTION

The very first time a subject is mentioned in the Bible it should be recognized as the most important truth about that subject, and serves as the key to understanding the fundamental and inherent meaning of that subject throughout Scripture.

SHADOWS AND TYPES

God speaks to us in pictures. In fact, the whole Bible is full of shadows and types, which are (mostly) pictures of Jesus and His Finished Work. The picture is the shadow and type and the substance (antitype) is the fulfillment in Jesus. When the Holy Spirit enlightens the picture in a flash of revelation understanding, true Biblical faith arises. Then we automatically speak and act from faith, and His power is released into our situation.

🔑 KEY CONCEPTS FOR GREEK GRAMMAR

It's essential to study the original text in the Greek and Hebrew to properly understand Scripture. Because the English doesn't have as much specificity of grammatical separation as other languages, it can lose some meaning in the translation, especially some of the looser, modern Bible translations which are more like Bible interpretations. The King Jas Version is one of the closest to the original text. Even so, Biblical Greek is difficult to misinterpret, and when we examine the original text, we can still draw out much clearer and deeper insight.

To properly translate and interpret the correct meaning from the original text it's important to study an interlinear Bible that reads from the original Greek or Hebrew, rather than one that reads from English.

We study word definitions and analyze form and punctuation of sentences. When you observe the root combinations that form individual words, the Koine Greek has especially rich understanding to uncover.

The Septuagint, which is the Old Testament translated into Koine Greek, is another tool that is helpful to understand how first century Christians interpreted the Hebrew.

GREEK VERBS

Use this tool as a reference to understand the form of the Greek verbs. Depending on their aspect they change the context and meaning. The basic aspects are person, number, voice, mood and tense.

PERSON *The subject of the verb*

FIRST PERSON The person *speaking* is the subject of the action, "*I* live."

SECOND PERSON The person being *spoken to* is the subject of the action, "*You* live."

THIRD PERSON The person being *spoken about* is the subject of the action, "*He* lives"

NUMBER *Singular or plural*

VOICE *Who is doing the action*

ACTIVE The subject is performing the action, e.g. *Jesus* was baptizing.

PASSIVE The subject is being acted upon or is the recipient of the action, e.g. *Jesus* was baptized by Jhn in the Jordan.

MIDDLE The subject is performing the action acting upon himself, e.g. *I* am washing myself.

MOOD

Mood deals with whether the statement is actual fact or only a possibility.

If the sentence is being stated as a fact, the mood reflects this regardless of whether it is true or false. **INDICATIVE** is the only mood conceived of as actual fact. In the other three moods, the action is thought of as possible or potential.

INDICATIVE A statement of fact or an actual occurrence from the writer's or speaker's perspective, e.g. "And they *overcame* him by the blood of the Lamb... (Rev 12:11)."

IMPERATIVE A command or instruction charging the hearer to perform a certain action, e.g. "*Flee* youthful lusts (2 Timothy 2:22)."

SUBJUNCTIVE indicates probability or possibility—the action of the verb *will possibly happen* depending on certain factors or circumstances. It is often used in conditional statements, i.e. if/then clauses.

However, if the subjunctive mood is used on a verb in a purpose or result clause, then the action should not be thought of as a possible result but as a definite outcome, e.g. "in order that now the manifold wisdom of God might be *made known* through the church... (Eph 3:10)."

OPTATIVE The mood of possibility is removed even further than the subjunctive. Often used to convey a wish or hope for a certain action to occur, e.g. "And the very God of peace sanctify you wholly; and I *pray* God your whole spirit and soul and body be preserved blameless unto the coming of our Lord Jesus Christ (1Th 5:23)."

TENSE

In most languages the tense of a verb refers to the **TIME OF THE ACTION**—present, past, or future. But in Greek, the primary consideration is the **KIND OF ACTION** that the verb portrays, and time is secondary.

The **KIND OF ACTION** will fall into one of three categories:

1. **CONTINUOUS** Progressive.
2. **COMPLETED** Accomplished with continuing results.
3. **SIMPLE** Summary or punctiliar occurrence without reference to progress. Simple doesn't always imply the action only happened at one point of time, but it is dependent on the meaning of the verb and other words in the context.

The only place in which the **TIME OF THE ACTION** comes to bear directly upon the tense of a verb is in the indicative mood. In all other moods the **KIND OF ACTION** is primary.

PRESENT Usually denotes continuous action in progress or a state of persistence. In the indicative mood, present tense denotes action going on in the present time, e.g. "in Whom you also *are being built* together into a dwelling place of God in spirit (Eph 2:22)."

AORIST Simple or summary occurrence without regard for the amount of time taken. Often referred to as punctiliar (single, one point-in-time action) although it may actually take place over a period of time. In the indicative mood, aorist tense denotes action that occurred in the past, and is often translated like the English simple past tense, e.g. "God... *made us alive together with* Christ (Eph 2:5)."

IMPERFECT Shows linear type of action going on for some extended period of time, continually or repeatedly in the past, e.g. "And with many such parables *He spoke (He kept speaking)* the word to them as they were able to hear it (Mk 4:33)." However, when the verb **1510 ΕΙΜΊ** "to be" is in the imperfect tense it should be considered a simple action happening in past time, e.g. "For *you were* once darkness, but now light in the Lord (Eph 5:8)."

PERFECT Unlike the English perfect tense which indicates a completed past action, the Greek perfect tense indicates an action that has been completed and the finished results are now in existence, continuing on in full effect. For example, Gal 2:20 should be translated "I am in a present state of having been crucified with Christ," indicating that not only was I crucified with Christ in the past, but I am existing now in that present condition.

FUTURE Just like the English future tense—an anticipated action or a certain happening that will occur in the future, e.g. "We know that if he is manifested, *we will be* like Him, for *we will see* Him even as He is (1Jhn 3:2)."

PLUPERFECT Past perfect shows action that is complete and existed at some time in the past indicated by the context. This tense is only found in the indicative mood and is rarely used in the New Testament, e.g. "All the angels *stood* around the throne and the elders and the four living creatures, and fell on their faces before the throne and worshiped God,... (Revelation 7:11)."

FUTURE PERFECT Much like pluperfect only the completed state will exist at some time in the future. Very rarely used in the New Testament. "And I will give you the keys of the kingdom of heaven, and whatever you bind on earth will *be bound* in heaven, and whatever you loose on earth will *be loosed* in heaven (Mat 16:19)."

GREEK NOUNS

NOMINATIVE The subject of the verb, "*He* went"

VOCATIVE The person(s) being directly addressed, "Jesus spoke to *him.*"

ACCUSATIVE The direct object of the verb, "They cast their *nets.*"

GENITIVE The one possessing the noun, "*His* word."

DATIVE The indirect object, instrument, or location, "Go to the *temple.*"

Key Concepts for Greek Grammar has been edited and used by permission ©New Creation Life Intl..

INTRODUCTION

THE PURSUIT

Every single person who has been washed by the blood of Christ can live a *Spirit-empowered life*[3]—a life endued with **supernatural power;**[3] an existence **strengthened by the might of God;**[3] a reality which defies the physical boundaries of this age. We see this truth in scriptures like Mark 16:17-18, yet sadly today, it's quite apparent the majority of the church **believes**[7] very little.

So, the burning question on the lips of those who **hunger and thirst**[7d] for everything that belongs to the *righteous in Christ*[8] (Mat 5:6) is, *"How do we walk*[12] *in the Spirit-empowered life?"*[3]

> And **these signs**[3] **will follow those who believe:**[7] in My name they will cast out demons; they will speak with new tongues; they will take up serpents; and if they drink anything deadly, it will by no means hurt them; they will lay hands on the sick, and they will recover." **MK16:17-18**
>
> Blessed are those who **hunger and thirst**[7d] for **righteousness;**[8] for they shall be filled. **MAT 5:6**

ACTIVATING THE FINISHED WORK IN US

It's astonishing to realize that everything Jesus accomplished through the Finished Work from the garden to the throne, the very power of our *salvation*[16] lies dormant and unappropriated without the **work of the Holy Spirit.**[3]

> Then Mary said, "Behold the maidservant of the Lord! **Let it be to me according to your word."**[7] And the angel departed from her. **LK 1:38**

When Jesus sat down at the right hand of the Father, He wasn't satisfied. Even though our salvation is finished, nobody benefits from it until the Holy Spirit unveils it by *revelation.*[10] The believer must respond with an *"Amen!"*[7] agreeing like Mary did when she was visited by the angel in Luke 1:38 saying, *"Let it be to me according to your word."*[7]

1

> Then, the same day at evening, being the first day of the week, when the doors were shut where the disciples were assembled, for fear of the Jews, Jesus came and stood in the midst, and said to them, "*Peace¹* be with you." **JHN 20:19**

On resurrection day, even the twelve disciples, His closest followers were behind closed doors for fear of the Jews (Jhn 20:19), not comprehending at all what had transpired at Calvary. It wasn't until the Holy Spirit caused the *light of revelation*¹⁰ to ignite their understanding that they began to *boldly walk*¹² in the empowerment of the *New Creation.*⁹

🏛 The two men on the road to Emmaeus were sad (Lk 24:17) until they had the Scriptures *revealed*¹⁰ to them (Lk 24:25-27, 30-35). The Holy Spirit *opened their eyes*¹⁰ and they recognized the living Christ as they took *communion,*¹⁹ the New Covenant ordinance by which we remember Him. The Spirit-empowered result was that they *witnessed to others*¹³ the *fresh revelation*¹⁰ of all the Old Covenant *shadows and types*¹⁹ that were revealed in, and by, the risen Christ.

> **17** And He said to them, "What kind of conversation is this that you have with one another as you walk and are sad?" ... **25** Then He said to them, "O foolish ones, and slow of heart to believe in all that the prophets have spoken! **26** Ought not the Christ to have suffered these things and to enter into His glory?" **27** And beginning at Moses and all the Prophets, *He expounded to them in all the Scriptures*¹³ the *things concerning Himself.*¹⁹ ... **30** Now it came to pass, as He sat at the table with them, that *He took bread, blessed and broke it, and gave it to them.*¹⁹ **31** Then *their eyes were opened*¹⁰ and they *knew Him;*¹⁰ and He vanished from their sight. **32** And they said to one another, "Did not our heart burn within us while He talked with us on the road, and while *He opened the Scriptures*¹⁰ to us?" **33** So they rose up that very hour and returned to Jerusalem, and found the eleven and those who were with them gathered together, **34** saying, "The Lord is risen indeed, and has appeared to Simon!" **35** And they told about the things that had happened on the road, and how *He was known to them*¹⁰ in the *breaking of bread.*¹⁹ **LK 24:17, 25-27, 30-35**

Peter before Pentecost was in denial and fear. Then filled with the Holy Spirit, he boldly stood up before the whole assembly and *spoke*

But Peter, standing up with the eleven, *raised his voice and said*[4a] to them, "Men of Judea and all who dwell in Jerusalem, let this be known to you, and heed my words. For these are not drunk, as you suppose, since it is only the third hour of the day. But *this is what was spoken by the prophet Joel:*[4a] 'And it shall come to pass in the last days, says God, that *I will pour out of My Spirit on all flesh;*[3a] your sons and your daughters shall *prophesy,*[4a] your young men shall see *visions,*[3e] your old men shall dream *dreams.*[3e] And on My menservants and on My maidservants I will pour out My Spirit in those days; And they shall prophesy. **ACTS 2:14-18**

the first prophecy[4a] of the New Covenant (Acts 2:14-17, whole story through v41). The Spirit-empowered result was that 3,000 were saved.

💧 Without Paul receiving *revelation*[10] for 14 years by no man but by the Holy Spirit, it's not unrealistic to say that none of us would even comprehend the work of the Cross or appropriate the New Creation at all (Gal 1:15-17, 2:1-2). *Nobody saw Jesus become sin for us on the Cross (2Cor 5:21); nobody saw* the blood sprinkled on the mercy seat in heaven (Heb 9:12); and *nobody saw* Him sit down at the right hand of the Father (Heb 1:3). All these truths were *revealed*[10] and eternalized through the Pauline epistles. Through these letters he has trained

But when it pleased God, who separated me from my mother's womb and called me through His grace, *to reveal His Son in me,*[10] that I might *preach Him*[13] among the Gentiles, I did not immediately confer with flesh and blood, nor did I go up to Jerusalem to those who were apostles before me; but I went to Arabia, and returned again to Damascus. **GAL 1:15-17**

Then after fourteen years I went up again to Jerusalem with Barnabas, and also took Titus with me. And *I went up by revelation,*[10] and communicated to them that *gospel*[1] which I *preach*[13] among the Gentiles... **GAL 2:1-2**

For He made Him who knew no sin to be sin for us, that we might become the *righteousness of God*[8] in Him. **2COR 5:21**

Not with the blood of goats and calves, but with His own blood He entered the Most Holy Place once for all, having obtained eternal redemption. **HEB 9:12**

who being the brightness of His glory and the express image of His person, and upholding all things by the word of His power, when He had by Himself purged our sins, *sat down at the right hand of the Majesty on high,*[1d] **HEB 1:3**

us all to move from Old Testament thinking to *New Covenant reality.*[1d] The Spirit-empowered result is that believers throughout the generations of the Church age have said *"Amen"*[7] to the truth and appropriated their salvation by faith.

What we don't know, we won't access (Rom 10:14-15). Conversely, the more we understand these truths, the more we'll partake of them. The *kingdom of heaven*[26a] becomes a reality to us when it's *preached,*[13] we receive the *revelation,*[10] faith arises and we respond with our *"Amen!"*[7] *Then* the Holy Spirit brings it to pass.

> How then shall they call on Him in whom they have not believed? And *how shall they believe*[7] *in Him of whom they have not heard?*[13] And how shall they hear without a preacher? And how shall they preach unless they are sent? As it is written: "How beautiful are the feet of those who preach the gospel of peace, Who bring glad tidings of good things!" **ROM 10:14-15**

In other words, after Pentecost, the Holy Spirit was given to implement every aspect of *salvation*[1e] in our life. Even though Jesus finished it completely, until the Holy Spirit activates and *empowers*[3] the Word of truth, *it has no actual effect in our life!*

Jesus is longing for us to say *"Yes"*[7] to every aspect of what He provided so the Holy Spirit can manifest our inheritance and bring it to pass in a practical way.

> If we live in the Spirit, *let us also walk*[12] *in the Spirit.*[2a] **GAL 5:25**
>
> **KEY GREEK WORD**
>
> **4043 PERIPATEÓ:**[12] (per-ee-pat-eh'-o) to walk. Hebraistically, to conduct my life, live. † From **4012 PERÍ,** comprehensively around, which intensifies **3961 PATÉŌ,** walk—properly, to walk around. *To regulate one's life.

Now it's up to us to *pursue Him.*[7d] But to truly understand what it means to *walk*[12] *in the Spirit*[2a] (Gal 5:25), it's important to make the connection between how we *walk out, conduct, or regulate our lives,*[12] not in a legalistic, behavioral sense but instead, by the empowering *breath of God.*[19]

4

THE FINE DISTINCTIONS OF THE BREATH OF GOD

The *breath of God*[19] is His *Spirit.*[3]
He *breathes His life*[19] into us and we become a *living soul*[17] that *breathes.*
The *life-force*[19] and *source of our breath* is the *breath and life of God*[19]

2222 ZÓÉ:[19] (dzo-ay') Life. † All life comes from, and is sustained by God.
*The vital spirit, the breath of life, a life preserved in the midst of perils,
with a suggestion of vigor, of the absolute fullness of life.

SPIRIT[3a]	BREATH[19]	SOUL[17]
The wind/breath from the outside.	The wind/breath from the inside.	The wind/breath that is life.
HEB 7307 RUACH: (roo'-akh) breath, wind, spirit.	**HEB 5397 NESHAMAH:** (nesh-aw-maw') breath	**HEB 5315 NEPHESH:** (neh'-fesh) a soul, living being, life, self, desire, emotion
GK 4151 PNEUMA: (pnyoo'-mah) wind, spirit, breath.	**GK 4157 PNOÉ:** (pno-ay') a blowing, wind, breath, gust, breeze.	**GK 5590 PSUCHÉ:** (psoo-khay') the soul, breath of life, the soul as the seat of affections and will. The root of English word, *psyche*.

WALKING IN THE WIND

Adam became a *living soul*[17] characterized by the *life of God,*[19] when he was *breathed to life*[19] by God the Father (Gen 2:7). Before the fall, he *walked*[12] *in the wind*[3a] with Him, which is the **7307 RUACH,**[3] or the Spirit (Gen 3:8). We could say Adam *conducted his life*[12] under the influence of the *breath of God.*[19]

Now, it's our choice whether we want to *"walk*[12] *in the wind*[3a]"* completely enveloped by the influence of the Spirit and *breath of God,*[19] or *conduct our lives*[12] hiding in the *fig leaves of*

And the LORD God formed man of the dust of the ground, and breathed into his nostrils the *breath of life;*[19] and man became a living *soul.*[17] **GEN 2:7**

7 Then the eyes of both of them were opened, and they knew that they were naked; and *they sewed fig leaves together and made themselves coverings.*[18a]
8 And they heard the sound of the LORD God *walking*[12] *in the garden in the cool of the day,*[3a] and Adam and his wife *hid themselves*[18a] from the presence of the LORD God among the trees of the garden. **GEN 3:7-8**

5

> how much more shall the blood of Christ, who through the eternal Spirit offered Himself without spot to God, cleanse your **conscience**[17c] **from dead works**[18a] to serve the living God? **HEB 9:14**

self-effort and dead works,[18a] overrun by the flesh and plagued by **sin consciousness**[17c] (Gen 3:8 p5, Heb 9:14, *The Finished Work of Christ;* Chapter 3).

No doubt, all of us would say we choose to walk in the wind, but we're typically oblivious to the fact that our automatic tendency is to blindly do the exact opposite. For this reason, it's crucial to identify how we fall into this trap. But first, let's note these connections about life, death and the breath of God:

Before receiving the **breath of God,**[19] Adam had *no life*[20] (Gen 2:7 p5).

The **written Word**[1c] lies in wait for the Spirit to breath upon it and bring forth the *life*[19] that's in it (2Cor 3:6).

Before we're **breathed to life**[19] in the new birth, we're **spiritually dead**[20] (Jhn 20:21-22, Eph 2:1-3).

Now we've been *made alive,*[19] **by the same power**[29] **Christ was raised**[14] from the dead, we're capable of **producing spiritual fruit**[3d] consistent with the **New Creation life**[9] of God (Rom 6:4).

> who also made us sufficient as ministers of the new covenant, not of the letter but of the Spirit; **for the letter kills,**[24] **but the Spirit gives life.**[19] **2COR 3:6**

> So Jesus said to them again, "Peace to you! As the Father has sent Me, I also send you." And when He had said this, **He breathed on them,**[19] and said to them, **"Receive the Holy Spirit.**[2] **JHN 20:21-22**

> And you He **made alive,**[19] who **were dead**[20] in trespasses and sins, in which you once **walked**[12] **according to the course of this world,**[27] according to the prince of the power of the air, the spirit who now works in the sons of disobedience, among whom also we all once conducted ourselves in the lusts of our flesh, fulfilling the desires of the flesh and of the mind, and were by nature children of wrath, just as the others. **EPH 2:1-3**

> Therefore we were buried with Him through baptism into death, that just as **Christ was raised**[14] from the dead by the glory of the Father, **even so**[29] we also **should walk**[12] in **newness of life.**[9] **ROM 6:4**

UNRAVELING A PRECONCEIVED IDEA:

WHAT IS LEGALISM?

👣 It's essential to highlight possibly the most fundamental key to walking in the power of the New Covenant and expose one of the **biggest deceptions of the enemy**[21] that has been arrayed against the church since the very beginning. What we typically have been taught is to try **to do everything right and improve ourselves in a legalistic way.**[18a] This is the polar opposite of what God has said.

Anything to do with us perfecting ourselves, by ourselves, is legalism, and according to Paul, it's grave foolishness (Gal 3:1-3)!

Rather, we are **empowered**[3] **to walk**[12] in **New Creation life**[9] by **revelation**[10] of who He has made us in Christ—**washed,**[1e] **empowered**[3] and **authorized sons of God,**[15] and it's the Spirit who is **renewing,**[17a] **sanctifying**[3c] and perfecting us.

> **O foolish Galatians! Who has bewitched you**[21] that you should not obey the truth, before whose eyes Jesus Christ was clearly portrayed among you as crucified? This only I want to learn from you: Did you **receive the Spirit**[2] by the **works of the law,**[24] or by the **hearing of faith?**[7] Are you so foolish? **Having begun in the Spirit,**[2] are you now **being made perfect**[3c] **by the flesh?**[18a] **GAL 3:1-3**

Now we view our surroundings and circumstances with **God's correct perspective.**[17a] How much **light**[10] we perceive determines how we automatically respond in all situations. We speak and act from **empowerment**[3] of His **leading,**[2a] from **revelation**[10] and **spiritual understanding,**[17a] which sets the supernatural course of our whole life.

<u>This</u> is walking in **Christian maturity,**[17a] and how God is able to use us for His **glory.**[3]

OUR PURPOSEFUL PURSUIT

As spiritual beings, we reside in a *corrupted*[20] *flesh*[18] in a fallen world—the result of *Adam's disobedience*[23] (Rom 5:12). But through submission to His leadership, we can be so influenced by the presence of His glory in us that our every thought, word and deed can not only be directed, but *supernaturally empowered*[3] by the *life*[19] of God (2Cor 4:16, Eph 6:10).

> Therefore, just as *through one man sin entered the world,*[23] and death through sin, and thus death spread to all men, because all sinned– **ROM 5:12**
>
> Therefore, we do not lose heart. Even though our *outward man*[18] is *perishing,*[20] yet the inward man is *being renewed*[17a] day by day. **2COR 4:16**
>
> Finally, my brethren, *be strong in the Lord and in the power of His might.*[3] **EPH 6:10**

KEY GREEK WORD

1311 DIAPHTHEIRÓ:[20] (dee-af-thi'-ro) Corrupt, in a constant state of decay.

Living in the fullness of the *Spirit-empowered life*[3] doesn't happen by accident, but by *purposeful pursuit*[7d] of *intimate relationship*[2a] with God the Father. It comes through the Holy Spirit to *our spirit in the inner man*[16] (Eph 3:16), all made possible by the blood of Christ.

> that He would grant you, according to the riches of *His glory,*[3] to be *strengthened with might*[3] through His Spirit in the *inner man,*[16] **EPH 3:16**
>
> Christ has redeemed us from the curse of the law, having become a curse for us (for it is written, "Cursed is everyone who hangs on a tree"), *that*[30] the blessing of Abraham might come upon the Gentiles in Christ Jesus, *that*[30] *we might receive the promise of the Spirit*[3a] through faith. **GAL 3:13-14**
>
> ... *work out*[3] your own *salvation*[1e] with fear and trembling; for *it is God who works in you*[3] both to will and *to do*[3] for His good pleasure. **PHL 2:12-13**

The restoration of *spiritual relationship*[2] with the Father is the whole foundation of the New Covenant and the entire reason Jesus carried out the Finished Work. We were washed by the blood *so that*[30] we could receive the *blessing of Abraham,*[8] *so that*[30] we qualify to be *filled by the Holy Spirit*[2] (Gal 3:13-14). This *relationship*[2] is cultivated and matured in *our inner man*[16] and results in the *out-*

working[3] of our *salvation*[1e] yielding supernatural fruit. Notice *it's God who works in us*[3] which results in an *outward action*[3] (Phl 2:12-13). *This* is the *Spirit-empowered life*[3] that we live from the *inside*[16] *out.*[3]

Through this book, we'll understand how we were created, what changed when *Adam fell,*[23] and how we've been *restored*[2] by God's plan of *redemption.*[1] Then, we'll be formally introduced to the person of the Holy Spirit through the depths of Scripture. What are all His names? What do the *shadows and types*[19] represent? What is His job description? What are His methods of communication? How does He *lead us and guide us into all truth?*[2a] What are the manifestations of His power?

> But God, who is rich in mercy, *because of His great love with which He loved us,*[1] even when we were dead in trespasses, made us alive together with Christ (by grace you have been saved), **EPH 2:4-5**
>
> As the deer pants for the water brooks, so pants my soul for You, O God. *My soul thirsts*[7d] for God, for the living God. When shall *I come and appear before God?*[2] **PS 42:1-2**
>
> but *whoever drinks*[7d] of the water that I shall give him will never thirst. But the water that I shall give him will become in him *a fountain of water springing up into everlasting life.*[4] **JHN 4:14**

As our *spiritual appetite*[7d] increases to continually perceive *His abiding presence,*[2] we'll be astonished to realize how God *yearns for us*[1] (Eph 2:4-5)! His objective is to lovingly woo us to *restoration of fellowship.*[2] As we experience the intoxication of this intimate communion, our heart will be captured by a *deep thirst*[7d] and *passionate surrender*[2a] to *spiritual oneness and face-to-face relationship*[2] (Ps 42:1-2).

He is our *everlasting fountain of new life,*[4] by whom we are perpetually satisfied (Jhn 4:14). Sown in *Biblical knowledge,*[1c] rooted in *revelation,*[10] and harvested in *wisdom,*[10] *spiritual understanding*[17a] and *power,*[3] our thirst for His *living water*[4] will become the perpetual longing of our soul.

9

ONE
LIVING OUT OF THE INNER MAN

he key to living out of our *inner man*[16] in accordance with our *new nature*[9] is discovered in fully realizing our makeup. Being eternally *reborn*[19] *in Christ,*[1e] yet still living in a *corrupted flesh*[18] poses very real challenges that very few believers properly understand. Typically, we have received many mixed messages and misinterpreted ideas about how to manage being *eternally redeemed,*[1e] yet *physically flawed,*[18] *spiritually perfected,*[16] yet *naturally bent.*[17b]

Between the two extremes of our *eternal spirit*[16] and *dying, corrupted flesh,*[18] our *soul*[17] is subject to whichever side has dominance. We can live *spiritually*[17a] or *carnally minded,*[17b] and we can alternate back and forth in any given moment (Rom 8:5-6, 7:21-25). The *fallen nature*[20] of the *flesh*[18] is always trying to entrap our *unregenerate thinking.*[17b] Whereas our *New Creation heart*[9] that has God's law written on it firmly

> For those who live according to the flesh set their minds on the things of the flesh, but those who live according to the Spirit, the things of the Spirit. For to be *carnally minded*[17b] is death, but to be *spiritually minded*[17a] is life and peace. **ROM 8:5-6**
>
> I find then a law, that evil is present with me, the one who wills to do good. For I delight in the law of God according to the inward man. But I see *another law in my members,*[18] warring against the law of my mind, and bringing me into captivity to the *law of sin which is in my members.*[18] O wretched man that I am! Who will deliver me from this body of death? I thank God—through Jesus Christ our Lord! So then, *with the mind*[17a] I myself serve the law of God, but *with the flesh*[18] the law of sin. **ROM 7:21-25**

desires to *yoke our mind*[17] to the *leadership of the Holy Spirit.*[2a] The prevailing side is determined first, by our *spiritual awareness,*[17a] and second, by our level of *submission to His leadership.*[2a] Spiritual thinking occurs when we connect our mind to the Holy Spirit. As we learn to allow Him to take control, He drives out the corruption in the *flesh*[18] and thoroughly *renovates our mind.*[17a] The result is we automatically produce the *fruit*[3d] of the root.

When *Adam fell*[23] from *eternal spirit-man,*[16] to *corrupted man*[20] separated from the life of God, his mind had to be renewed to death. In the opposite way, we must be *renewed*[17a] to the *eternal life of God*[19] that is within us. We haven't even begun to comprehend the significance of the *power*[3] that is in *our spirit in our inner man*[16] which enables us to live spiritually. By understanding the difference between us and Adam, we'll be better equipped to cooperate with the purpose of God.

FROM ADAM TO US—A PICTURE OF OPPOSITES

Just like Adam was, we are a *spirit-being,*[16] we have a *soul,*[17] and we live in a *body.*[18] But in contrast, we came into the world in the *fallen state*[20] *that Adam left in.* Let's look at the similarities and differences:

> <u>Born into death,</u>[20] our *bodies*[18] are made from the *same cursed elements of the cursed earth.*[20] We are intimately acquainted with death from birth, to the extent that we struggle to comprehend a *perfected, eternal flesh.*[18b] This is the reason it's challenging for our *minds*[17] to appropriate supernatural *healing*[5] by *faith;*[7]

> <u>Adam was created with no concept of death</u>[20] and it took 930 years for his mind to be completely renewed to *physical death.*[18] He didn't know what *"old"* or *"sick"* was until ever-so-gradually, he experienced it and he *physically died.*[18]

> <u>We are born with no comprehension of life</u>[19] <u>or unity with God.</u>[2] Without the forgiveness of sins by the blood of Christ we would have remained that way. Even now that we've been restored, *intimacy and fellowship with God*[2] is

not automatically perceived. Developing our ability to be *continually aware of God*[2a] and what He's saying moment by moment must be *purposefully pursued*[7d] (Introduction), and *is the subject of this whole book;*

Adam was intimately acquainted with God[2] from the moment he was created. Relationship and seeing the world from the *divine perspective*[2] was automatic for him.

⬥ Now that we've been redeemed, we urgently need the *light to shine in our understanding to comprehend*[10] our *restored life*[19] and fellowship with God.[2] If we were to allow the *renewing of our mind*[17a] to *life*[19] (Rom 12:2) to take as long as Adam's *mind*[17] was renewed to *death*[20] (930 years old when he died), we will never experience the fullness of our *salvation*[1e] here on earth. We would perish for *lack of knowledge*[10b] long before (Hos 4:6).

> And do not be conformed to this world, but *be transformed by the renewing of your mind,*[17a] that you may prove what is that good and acceptable and perfect will of God. **ROM 12:2**
>
> My people are destroyed for *lack of knowledge*[10b]... **HOS 4:6**

So learning to truly *submit to the Holy Spirit*[2a] through the Word of God is how we start living *out of our inner man.*[16] Taking hold of our *relationship of oneness with God*[2] starts here.

A GLIMPSE INTO ADAM'S NATURE

Adam opened his eyes in the midst of a intimate moment—the *breath of God*[19] awakening him to become a *living soul*[17] (Gen 2:7).

> And the Lord God formed man of the dust of the ground, and *breathed into his nostrils*[19] the *breath of life;*[19] and man became a *living soul.*[17] **GEN 2:7 KJV**

Being a living soul meant that as a *spiritual being,*[16] he had an *intellectual mind*[17] that could reason, a *free will*[17] that made choices

12

> And they were both naked, the man and his wife, and were not ashamed. **GEN 2:25**
>
> What is man that You are mindful of him, And the son of man that You visit him? For You have made him a little lower than the angels, And You have **crowned him with glory**[3a] and **honor.**[3f] **PS 8:4-5**
>
> Then God said, "Let Us make man in **Our image, according to Our likeness;**[9] let them **have dominion**[15] over the fish of the sea, over the birds of the air, and over the cattle, over all the earth and over every creeping thing that creeps on the earth." **GEN 1:26**

and decisions, and **emotions**[17] that caused conscious feelings as he experienced God's creation.

More than that, Adam was a soul completely influenced by the **life of God.**[19] His **thought life**[17] was consumed by **God's perspective**[17a] and he perceived everything from His **divine viewpoint,**[17a] yet he still had a free will.

Adam was naked and felt no shame (Gen 2:25) because he was **clothed in the glory of God**[3a] (Ps 8:4-5, *The Finished Work of Christ;* Chapter 2). He had the Spirit **on him**[3a] **and in him**[2] (Chapter 3), and he was endued with **power**[3] and **authority**[15] (Gen 1:26). He was **honored**[3f] above every other creation, even the angels.

Adam was made in **God's image**[9] and created to live forever. He was in perfect **Spirit-to-spirit relationship**[2] with the creator of heaven and earth.

ADAM'S FALL

When Adam sinned, the awful pronouncement of God from Genesis 2:17 came to pass, "in the day you eat, **dying**[20] **you shall die**[20]..." *Two deaths!*

> but of the tree of the knowledge of good and evil you shall not eat, for in the day that you eat of it you shall **surely**[20] **die.**[20] **GEN 2:17**
>
> **KEY HEBREW WORD**
>
> **4191 MUTH:**[20] (mooth) to die
>
> In Genesis 2:17, **4191 MUTH**, is repeated twice—two deaths.

💧 Just imagine that day from Adam's perspective:

In one horrible, instantaneous moment *he fell*[23] from his status as a

> *in Him*[1] was *life,*[19] and the life was the *light*[10] of men. And the light shines in the *darkness,*[20] and the *darkness did not comprehend it.*[20] **JHN 1:4-5**

god-class creation, in perfect *Spirit-to-spirit oneness*[2] with the Father, consumed by the *life*[19] and *light*[10] of God. Now, he was a *natural creation spiritually separated from God.*[20] With a Spirit-to-soul standing, Adam was overtaken by a *spiritual darkness that could not comprehend*[20] the *light*[10] anymore (Jhn 1:4-5, Chapter 9).

TWO DEATHS

The first death was the instant *spiritual death.*[20] Still an eternal *spirit man,*[16] but spiritually dead by being *completely cut off from God,*[20] the branch severed from the vine. He couldn't *walk*[12] with Him in the *evening breeze,*[3] or rather, *the Spirit*[3] (Gen 3:8). He couldn't *reason with Him or relate to Him*[2] in any way.

> And they heard the sound of the Lord God walking in the garden in the *cool [afternoon breeze] of the day,*[3] so the man and his wife hid and kept themselves hidden from the presence of the Lord God among the trees of the garden. **GEN 3:8 AMP**
>
> **KEY HEBREW WORD**
>
> **7307 RUACH:**[3] (roo'-akh) breath, wind, *spirit.*

The second death was the *slow physical death.*[18] Adam was made from the dust of the earth and just as *the curse*[20] permeated into the earth, it permeated Adam's body. The slow process of *"dust-to-dust"*[20] had begun. The branch separated from the source of *life*[19] began to decay.

> But the Lord God called to Adam, and said to him, "Where are you?" He said, "I heard the sound of You [walking] in the garden, and *I was afraid*[21] because I was *naked;*[20] so I hid myself." **GEN 3:9-10 AMP**

🜄 In the blink of an eye, the two deaths changed him from an *incorruptible spirit-man*[16] to *corrupted;*[20] from *physically eternal*[18b] to *temporal.*[18] Now he was *naked,*[20] *ashamed,*[21] and plagued with a new formidable torment of his soul—*fear*[21] (Gen 3:9-10).

All Adam had left was a mere memory of *precious unity*[2] with the God of all creation, which would fade over time in the same way our memories of childhood grow dim and distant.

He was banned from the garden by *saving grace*[5]—if they had eaten from the *tree of life*[19] while in this awful condition of death and separation, mankind would have been *cursed*[20] for all eternity with no hope of *redemption*[1] (*The Finished Work of Christ;* Chapters 2 & 3).

LESSON 4

THE NATURE OF OUR SALVATION IN THE CURRENT AGE

Understanding the fall of Adam, we can get a glimpse of our current state, but in reverse. Let's continue to look at the picture of opposites:

Adam fell[23] from *walking*[12] *with God*[2] to walking in the presence of the enemy;

We were raised up[15] from walking according to the prince of the power of the air, to *walking*[12] in the *presence and power of God*[2] through the Holy Spirit (Eph 2:1-2, 6).

We were offspring of Adam,[20] children of the disobedient one (Eph 2:1-2);

Now we have been born of the Spirit[19] of an *incorruptible seed*[9] and we are *sons of God*[15] (Jhn 3:5-6, 1Pet 1:23).

And you *He made alive,*[19] who were *dead in trespasses and sins,*[20] in which you once *walked*[12] according to the course of this world, according to the prince of the power of the air, the spirit who now works in the sons of disobedience, **EPH 2:1-2**

and *raised us up together, and made us sit together in the heavenly places in Christ Jesus,*[15] **EPH 2:6**

Jesus answered, "Most assuredly, I say to you, unless one is *born of water and the Spirit,*[19] he cannot enter the kingdom of God. That which is born of the flesh is flesh, and that which is *born of the Spirit*[19] is spirit. **JHN 3:5-6**

having been *born again,*[19] not of corruptible seed but *incorruptible,*[9] through the *Word of God*[1c] which *lives and abides forever,*[2] **1 PET 1:23**

We had the Adamic nature of death; [20]

Now we have been quickened, or made alive [19] (Eph 2:1-2 p15), which means an actual resurrection from death has happened in our *spirit,* [16] and we have the *nature of God.* [9]

We were compelled to conduct ourselves [12] *according to the lust of the flesh,* [18] and sin had dominion over us;

Now we are slaves to righteousness [9] having His law written on our *New Creation heart.* [9] (Rom 6:18). Having God's nature, doing good is now our inward desire and every time we sin we actually have to rebel against our own heart to do it.

> And having been set free from sin, you became *slaves of righteousness.* [9]
> **ROM 6:18**

According to his *inner fallen man, Adam did evil works;* [20a]

We live according to our *redeemed nature* [9] and *by His workmanship, we are created in Christ to do good works.* [2a] (Eph 2:10, Chapter 14)

> *For we are His workmanship, created in Christ Jesus for good works,* [2a] which God prepared beforehand that we should walk in them. **EPH 2:10**

UNRAVELING A PRECONCEIVED IDEA:

WALKING ACCORDING TO THE FLESH

It's essential to understand that *walking* [12] *according to the flesh* [18] is not doing sins, in and of itself (Rom 8:5). Rather, it is putting *confidence in our own*

> For those who live *according to the flesh* [18] set their *minds* [17] on the things of the flesh, but those who *live according to the Spirit,* [2a] the things of the Spirit. **ROM 8:5**

strength and ability;[18a] being led by our *natural senses*[17b] that cause us to walk by sight, not by faith; and thinking in our own *natural reasoning*[17b] which is constantly being infiltrated by the *calculated arguments*[21] of the devil (Phl 3:3, 2Cor 5:7, Eph 4:17, 2Cor 10:5).

Walking[12] *according to the flesh*[18a] will ultimately lead to doing the *works of the flesh*[20a] (Gal 5:19-21), however fleshly living is essentially *conducting our life*[12] in *self-empowered, self-willed and natural behavior*[18a] that is void of relationship with God.

For we are the circumcision, who worship God in the Spirit, rejoice in Christ Jesus, and *have no confidence in the flesh,*[1d] **PHL 3:3**

For we walk by faith, not by sight. **2COR 5:7**

This I say, therefore, and testify in the Lord, that you should *no longer walk as the rest of the Gentiles walk, in the futility of their mind,*[17b] **EPH 4:17**

casting down arguments[21] and every high thing that exalts itself against the knowledge of God, bringing every thought into captivity to the obedience of Christ, **2COR 10:5**

Now the *works of the flesh*[20] are evident, which are: adultery, fornication, uncleanness, lewdness, idolatry, sorcery, hatred, contentions, jealousies, outbursts of wrath, selfish ambitions, dissensions, heresies, envy, murders, drunkenness, revelries, and the like... **GAL 5:19-21**

We *all* have an automatic tendency to *walk*[12] *according to the flesh.*[18a] Even though we have *His nature*[9] now, we were born into, and trained by the *corrupted nature.*[20] Separated from God, this nature always wants to religiously fix itself, by itself. It wants to *establish its own righteousness*[18d] rather than *submit to God's*[8] (Rom 10:3-4, *The Finished Work of Christ;* Chapter 3).

For they being ignorant of *God's righteousness,*[8] and *seeking to establish their own righteousness,*[18a] have not submitted to the righteousness of God. For *Christ is the end*[1] *of the law for righteousness*[24] to everyone who *believes.*[7] **ROM 10:3-4**

> Stand fast therefore in the liberty wherewith Christ hath made us free, and be not entangled again with the yoke of bondage. Behold, I Paul say unto you, that if ye be circumcised, **Christ shall profit you nothing.**[18a] For I testify again to every man that is circumcised, that he is a debtor to do the whole law. **Christ is become of no effect unto you, whosoever of you are justified by the law; ye are fallen from grace.**[18a] **GAL 5:1-4 KJV**

Walking[12] *according to the flesh*[18a] (self-empowered effort, not sinful behavior) causes us to *fall from grace*[18a] where we live subject to the *curse that is in the earth and flesh*[20] (Gal 5:1-4). We don't lose our eternal salvation, but we do lose our access to the supernatural empowerment to live the Christian life. We are left to live by our own *self-effort*[18a] and we'll get natural results (*The Finished Work of Christ;* Chapter 7).

The whole purpose of this book is to saturate our understanding so we'll come to recognize when we unknowingly *walk*[12] *according to the flesh*[18a] and instead, learn to *live according to the Spirit.*[2a]

So as you read this next section (and this whole book), be sure to read it through this lens:

> Therefore, leaving the discussion of the elementary principles of Christ, let us go on to perfection, not laying again the foundation of repentance from **dead works**[18a] and of faith toward God, **HEB 6:1**

🦶 Flesh = our natural man that tends towards *self-empowered works, natural thinking and self-willed living*[18a] outside of intimacy with God. The self works we do are referred to in the Bible as *dead works*[18a] (Heb 6:1, *Total Saturation in the Spirit-Empowered Life:* Vol 2; Chapter 8).

LIVING ACCORDING TO OUR NEW NATURE IN THE INNER MAN

Salvation[1e] and the *restoration of spiritual relationship,*[2] is in the *inner man,*[16] not in the *outer man.*[18] Even so, it affects our *corrupted flesh*[18] with *life.*[19] Yet, it takes our cooperation.

> For those who live **according to the flesh**[18a] set their **minds on the things of the flesh,**[17b] but those who **live according to the Spirit,**[2a] the things of the Spirit. For to be **carnally minded**[17b] is **death,**[20] but to be **spiritually minded**[17a] is **life**[19] and **peace.**[1] Because the carnal mind is **enmity against God;**[20] for it is not subject to the law of God, nor indeed can be. So then, those who are in the flesh cannot please God. But **you are not in the flesh**[18] **but in the Spirit,**[2a] if indeed the Spirit of God dwells in you. Now if anyone does not have the Spirit of Christ, he is not His. **ROM 8:5-9**

In any given moment, knowingly or unknowingly, we will either obey the devil through our **flesh,**[18] or the Lord through our **spirit.**[16] We can give in to the constant demands and strong desires of the flesh and allow ourselves to be tossed about by **carnal thinking**[17b] which produces **death.**[20] Or we can learn to listen to our **spirit**[16] which is in **perfect union with His Spirit**[2] (Rom 8:5-9). The choice is ours.

When we were still sinners, <u>we had no choice</u> **but to act according to the fallen nature.**[20] Now we're in Christ, we don't automatically know how to live the Spirit-empowered life under the **leadership of the Spirit.**[2a] <u>We must choose to learn</u> how to live according to our new nature.[9]

Ephesians 4:17-19 shows us we could still **walk out our lives**[12] just like the unredeemed—in **emptiness of reasoning,**[17b] in **darkness of understanding, separated from intimacy with the life of God!**[20]

Not that He would alienate Himself from us. God the Father went to the ultimate lengths to justify us and **reconcile us to Himself**[1] eternally—nothing can undo what we have received by the blood of Christ (2Cor 5:19). But from **ignorance,**[10b] we can be

This I say, therefore, and testify in the Lord, that you should **no longer walk**[12] as the rest of the Gentiles walk, in the **futility of their mind,**[17b] having their **understanding darkened, being alienated from the life of God,**[20] because of the **ignorance**[10b] that is in them, because of the **blindness of their heart;**[20] who, being past feeling, have given themselves over to lewdness, to work all uncleanness with greediness. **EPH 4:17-19**

that is, that **God was in Christ reconciling the world to Himself,**[1] not imputing their trespasses to them... **2COR 5:19**

spiritually blind,[20] void of *spiritual relationship*[2] and *empowerment,*[3] and end up subject to sinful behavior.

In Romans 6:6, we see the *old man is dead.*[9] Having been crucified with Christ, we have put off the old man once and for all. Yet even so, the *corruption that is in the flesh*[18] still tries to find expression. This is why it's possible to have the *new nature,*[9] *created in true righteousness and holiness,*[8] and yet, still give ourselves over to the fallen state of the flesh that produces sin (Eph 4:20-24).

> Knowing this, that *our old man is crucified with him,*[9] that the *body of sin*[18] might be destroyed, that henceforth we should not serve sin. **ROM 6:6 KJV**
>
> But you have not so learned Christ, if indeed you have heard Him and have been taught by Him, as the truth is in Jesus: *that you put off, concerning your former conduct, the old man*[20] which grows corrupt according to the deceitful lusts, and *be renewed in the spirit of your mind,*[17a] and that you put on *the new man*[9] which was created according to God, in true *righteousness and holiness.*[8] **EPH 4:20-24**

> I say then: *Walk*[12] *in the Spirit,*[2a] and you shall not fulfill *the lust of the flesh.*[18] **GAL 5:16**

As we learn what it means to live out of our inner man and *walk*[12] *in the Spirit,*[2a] we won't fulfill the *strong desires and demands of the flesh*[18] (Gal 5:16). Instead, we'll be *renewed in the spirit of our mind*[17a] and *put no confidence in the flesh.*[18a]

LESSON 5

EMPOWERED BY OURSELVES OR EMPOWERED BY GOD

Living according to our *new nature*[9] doesn't mean we should try to become better Christians by indulging the desire to *battle our flesh in our own power.*[18a] This is the definition of *the natural-empowered life.*[18a] Worse than that, trying to fix the flesh, by the flesh, we come back under the law and *make Christ of no effect*[18a] (Gal 5:1-4).

👣 Instead we must *stand fast in the liberty wherewith Christ has made us free,*[1] become sensitive to listen to our *New Creation heart*[9] that always knows the right thing to do, and eagerly *surrender to the leadership of*

Stand fast therefore in the liberty wherewith Christ hath made us free,[1] and be not entangled again with the yoke of bondage. Behold, I Paul say unto you, that if ye be circumcised, Christ shall profit you nothing. For I testify again to every man that is circumcised, that he is a debtor to do the whole law. *Christ is become of no effect unto you, whosoever of you are justified by the law; ye are fallen from grace.[18a]* **GAL 5:1-4 KJV**

the Holy Spirit [2a] in our inner man (Chapter 2). Having developed our spiritual senses to the extent that we view our day-to-day world with *constant spiritual perception,[17a]* we live *spiritually-minded[17a]* (Rom 8:5-9 p19, *Total Saturation in the Spirit-Empowered Life:* Vol 2; Chapter 3). Every time we say *"yes"* to God's nature inside of us, He empowers us to *walk in it,[12]* and by definition, we truly are *sons of God[15]* (Rom 8:14-17).

For as many as are *led by the Spirit of God,[2a] these are sons of God.[15]* For you did not receive the spirit of bondage again to fear, but you received the Spirit of adoption by whom we cry out, "Abba, Father." The Spirit Himself bears witness with our spirit that we are children of God, and if children, then heirs—heirs of God and *joint heirs with Christ,[15]* if indeed we suffer with Him, that we may also be glorified together. **ROM 8:14-17**

Jesus answered and said to him, "Most assuredly, I say to you, unless one is born again, he cannot *see[10]* the *kingdom of God."[26a]* **JHN 3:3**

Your kingdom come. Your will be done *on earth as it is in heaven.[26a]* **MAT 6:10**

The Holy Spirit works in us and through us to the extent that we *submit to His leadership,[2a]* we become *partakers of the divine nature[9]* (2Pet 1:2-4, p24) and we will *see[10]* the *kingdom of God on earth, as it is in heaven[26a]* (Jhn 3:3, Mat 6:10).

This is the *Spirit-empowered life![3]*

PARTAKERS BY FAITH

In order to partake of the supernatural Spirit-empowered life, we have to *comprehend[10]* and *believe[7]* what has been given to us through *the Finished Work,[1]* and access His *grace provisions[5a]* by *faith[7]* (Rom 5:2).

through whom also we have *access by faith[7]* into this *grace[5a]* in which we *stand,[12]* and rejoice in *hope[31]* of the *glory of God.[3]* **ROM 5:2**

First, it's essential to adjust what we typically understand *faith*[7] to be and how we *"have it."*

UNRAVELING A PRECONCEIVED IDEA:

BELIEVING VS FAITH

When we declare, that we *believe*[7] the Word of God is forever settled

> Forever, O LORD, Your word is settled in heaven. **PS 119:89**

in heaven (Ps 119:89), we've made a final decision that whatever it says, we believe it, even if we don't fully comprehend it yet. We believe the Bible is God's final authority on all matters.

Typically, we think this is the definition of *faith,*[7] and we stop here.

However, what happens to our peace when our circumstances don't line up with what God has said? Do we question Him? Do we cry out to Him in despair, wondering why He's not *doing* His Word? Do we wonder what *we might have done* to stop His flow of blessing?

No condemnation—we've all been subject to this *carnal mindset*[17b] because it's the *devil's 24/7 job*[21] to keep us thinking like this. Yet, if this is our response, it sheds a harsh light on our *"faith"*[7] and clearly, we don't fully understand life in the New Covenant —yet (see *The Finished Work of Christ*; Chapter 11).

First, we must realize *the whole world is under the sway of the wicked one,*[20] so if our circumstances don't currently line up, it doesn't negate what God has said. We just haven't enforced *the victory Christ has won*[1] and appropriated part of our inheritance—yet.

👣 True Biblical *faith*[7] is not the same as *believing.*[7a] In fact, we can't make ourselves have faith. Rather, true faith is evidenced by the *automatic divine response*[7a] of actions and words that originate in our inner man as we *perceive what the Holy Spirit is saying*[4] about the Word right now (Rom 10:17 p25). In a *flash of revelation light*[10] He opens the eyes of our understanding about *Scripture;*[1c] about our *inheritance;*[1i] about *who we are in Christ.*[8] Then whatever we do and say from that revelation has *His power*[3] in it.

To live in *faith*[7] we need the Holy Spirit to *continually illuminate*[10] *the Word.*[1c] In our restored Spirit-to-spirit relationship, we can have it! The instant we truly *believe we've received,*[7b] it will come to pass (Mk 11:23-24).

> For assuredly, I say to you, whoever says to this mountain, 'Be removed and be cast into the sea,' and does not doubt in his heart, but *believes that those things he says will be done,*[7] he will have whatever he says. Therefore I say to you, whatever things you ask *when you pray, believe that you receive them,*[7b] and *you will have them.*[3] MK 11:23-24

RHÉMA VS LOGOS

4487 RHÉMA:[4] (hray'-mah) Word, *saying, utterance,* matter, command. ‡ Derived from the verb **4483 RHEO** "to speak" or "to say." *Emphasizes the spoken word as opposed to the written word*[1c] **(3056 LOGOS)**. Rhéma can denote a particular statement or command, often with a focus on its immediate impact or relevance. † *A spoken word, made "by the living voice"* (J. Thayer). *Commonly used in the NT for the Lord speaking His dynamic, living word in a believer to inbirth faith.*

3056 LOGOS:[1c] (log'-os) Word, speech, message, *account, reason, doctrine.* ‡ Derived from the Greek verb **3004 LEGŌ**, meaning "to speak" or "to say." In the New Testament, **"LOGOS"** is used to denote the spoken or *written word, the message of the Gospel,* and a title for Jesus Christ, emphasizing His role as the divine Word of God incarnate. Theologically, **"LOGOS"** signifies *the communication of God's will and truth to humanity.* The established principles of the kingdom of God.

‡ Berean Strong's Lexicon, † Helps Word-Studies

THE DIVINE NATURE THAT PRODUCES POWER AND VIRTUE

God's divine nature has changed us[9] completely, inside and out, yet we only *comprehend*[10] the tiniest fraction of who we are in Him (2Pet 1:2-4). A glorious incentive for us to pursue Him with all our heart, the more we *intimately know Christ*[2] and *Him crucified,*[1] the more *grace and peace is multiplied*[5] to us.

> *Grace and peace be multiplied*[5] to you in the *knowledge of God and of Jesus our Lord,*[2] as His *divine power*[3] has given to us all things that pertain to *life*[19] and *godliness,*[3d] through the knowledge of Him who called us by *glory*[3] and *virtue,*[3d] by which have been given to us exceedingly *great and precious promises,*[5a] that through these you may be *partakers of the divine nature,*[9] having escaped the corruption that is in the world through lust. **2PET 1:2-4**

In other words, as we seek deeper *revelation*[10] *of the Finished Work of Christ,*[1] the more we'll *partake of the divine nature.*[9] We'll escape the corruption that is in the world through the strong desire of the flesh—we'll completely come out from under it's influence.

We've been given everything we need to *walk*[12] in *life*[19] and *godliness,*[3d] and we've been called by *glory*[3] and *virtue:*[3d]

> *Life*[19] *and glory*[3] = the power of God on the inside that produces the miraculous.

> *Godliness and virtue*[3d] = the outward behavior that is the response from submitting to His leadership and doing the *good works*[2a] He preordained we should *walk in*[12] (Eph 2:10).

Typically, we have no idea how to

> For we are *His workmanship,*[2a] created in Christ Jesus for *good works,*[2a] which God prepared beforehand that we should *walk in them.*[12] **EPH 2:10**

> I will give you a new heart and put a new spirit within you; I will take the heart of stone out of your flesh and *give you a heart of flesh.*[9] I will put My Spirit within you and *cause you to walk*[12] *in My statutes,*[9] and you will keep My judgments and do them. Then you shall dwell in the land that I gave to your fathers; you shall be My people, and I will be your God. **EZ 36:26-28**

submit ourselves under His leadership.[2a] Up until now, we've probably equated submission as some version of us *trying to be better in our behavior.*[18a] However, *self-empowered effort*[18a] to do good things has no part in the Spirit-empowered life (Chapter 5). Instead, by the *New Creation heart,*[9] *He causes us to walk*[12] *in His statutes*[9] (Ez 36:26-28).

> So then faith comes by *hearing*[4] and *hearing*[4] by the (RHÉMA) *word*[4] of God.[1] ROM 10:17
>
> **KEY GREEK WORDS**
>
> **189 AKOÉ:**[4] (ak-o-ay') hearing. † Inner (spiritual) hearing, *discerning God's voice.*
>
> **5547 CHRISTOS:**[1] (khris-tos') The Anointed One, Messiah, Christ. † From **5548 XRÍŌ,** "anoint with olive oil."

The more *revelation light*[10] we seek and *spiritually perceive*[4] from the RHÉMA *Word of the Holy Spirit*[4] *about Christ,*[1] the more *faith*[7] will automatically arise (Rom 10:17).

Still referring to 2 Peter 1:2-4, the *life*[19] of God produces the *glorious resurrection power*[3] of the Holy Spirit from within us. The more we submit to His leadership, the more *godliness*[3d] and *virtue*[3d] we'll pour out—the root will produce the *fruit!*[3d]

FLIPPING THE SWITCH

> But you have an *anointing*[2a] from the Holy One, and you know all things. **1JHN 2:20**
>
> But the *anointing*[2a] which you have received from Him *abides in you,*[2a] and you do not need that anyone teach you; but as the same anointing teaches you concerning all things, and is true, and is not a lie, and *just as it has taught you, you will abide in Him.*[2a] **1JHN 2:27**

As we learn to *live out of*[12] our *inner man*[16] by the *renewing of our mind,*[17a] we'll receive revelation about the *anointing*[2a] that we now have (1Jhn 2:20, 27, Chapters 3 & 5). *Yielding to His power,*[3] we'll eagerly lay hands on the sick, and stand up in our *authority*[15] against every demonic oppression. We'll come to absolutely *expect*[31] the power of God to change our circumstances and the lives of those around us.

TWO

THE PARACLETE

Among many other names and descriptions in our English Bible, the Holy Spirit has been called *the Helper, the Comforter, the Counselor, the Advocate*—all of which are different translations of the same Greek word, **3875 PARÁKLĒTOS**.[2a] Transliterated into English we get the word *Paraclete*.[2a]

> **KEY GREEK WORD**
> **3875 PARÁKLETOS:**[2a] (par-ak'-lay-tos) called to one's aid, an advocate, intercessor, a consoler, comforter, helper, *Paraclete*. ‡ Someone called to aid, support, or intercede on behalf of another. Lawyer or legal counselor. † From **3844 PARÁ**, close-beside and **2564 KALÉŌ**, make a call, a legal advocate who makes the right judgment-call because they are close enough to the situation.

Looking at this compound word, made from **3844 PARÁ** (close beside) and **2564 KALÉŌ** (make a judgment call), it gives us an accurate description of the one who has been *called alongside*[2a] us to lead us and guide us into all truth (Jhn 16:13).

But just how close is He?

A *para*site attaches itself to drain and *feed off the life force* of its host.

> However, when He, the Spirit of truth, has come, He will *guide you into all truth;*[2a]... **JHN 16:13**

Our *Para*clete is so united with us as to infill, overshadow, and utterly *saturate us with His life*[19] *and power.*[3] This is, or rather, *we are His heavenly calling*—His very purpose and assignment in this church age!

We should ask ourselves, how much of His assignment are we submitting to and appropriating in our everyday lives? Not nearly enough. In fact, we will never come to the end of realizing the divine

‡ Berean Strong's Lexicon, † Helps Word-Studies

purpose and *ability*[3] available to us right now from being *yoked together*[2a] with the third person of the Godhead, the Holy Spirit. But it starts with a desire and *willing submission.*[2a]

TRADING OUR YOKE

🜊 A yoke is a wooden bar that fits over the shoulders of two work animals to join them together in order to share a heavy load. This shadow and type is

> Now therefore, why do you test God by putting a *yoke on the neck of the disciples which neither our fathers nor we were able to bear?*[24] ACTS 15:10

used throughout Scripture to depict both *partnership*[2] and *burden.*[24]

Being *yoked to the law*[24] is a burdensome load, utterly impossible to bear (Acts 15:10). It requires perfection, or death.

The whole reason Jesus was sent by the Father was to release us out of

> "The *Spirit of the Lord is upon Me,*[3a] because He has *anointed*[2a] Me to preach the *gospel*[1] to the poor; He has sent Me to heal the brokenhearted, to proclaim *liberty*[1] to the *captives*[20] and *recovery of sight*[10] to the *blind,*[20] to set at *liberty*[1] those who are *oppressed;*[20] to proclaim the *acceptable year of the Lord.*"[1d] LK 4:18-19

> Come to Me, all you who *labor*[18a] and are heavy laden, and I will give you *rest.*[1d] Take *My yoke*[2a] upon you and *learn*[2a] from Me, for I am gentle and lowly in heart, and you will find *rest*[1d] for your souls. For *My yoke is easy and My burden is light.*"[2a] MAT 11:28-30

> that if you *confess with your mouth the Lord Jesus and believe in your heart*[7] that God has raised Him from the dead, you will be *saved.*[1e] For *with the heart one believes*[7] unto righteousness,[8] and *with the mouth confession is made*[7] unto salvation.*[1e] ROM 10:9-10

this *bondage*[24] and bring us into *liberty*[1] (Lk 4:18-19). He beckoned every one of us to lay down the *heavy yoke of the law of sin and death,*[24] by taking up *His yoke which is easy and light*[2a] (Mat 11:28-30).

The rest we find is *the rest of the New Covenant*[1d] —by *His Finished Work,*[1] our death sentence has been paid and we are free from the *penalty of sin*[20] if we have *believed and confessed*[7] Jesus as our Lord and Savior (Rom 10:9-10).

> I will give you a *new heart*[9] and put a *new spirit*[16] within you; I will take the heart of stone out of your flesh and give you a *heart of flesh.*[9] **EZ 36:26**
>
> But this is the *covenant*[1] that I will make with the house of Israel after those days, says the Lord: *I will put My law in their minds, and write it on their hearts;*[9] and I will be their God, and they shall be My people. **JER 31:33**
>
> There is therefore now no condemnation to those who are in Christ Jesus, who do not *walk according to the flesh,*[18a] but *according to the Spirit.*[2a] For the *law of the Spirit of life in Christ Jesus*[2] has made me free from the *law of sin and death.*[24] **ROM 8:1-2**
>
> clearly you are an epistle of Christ, ministered by us, *written not with ink but by the Spirit of the living God,*[2a] not on *tablets of stone*[24] but on *tablets of flesh, that is, of the heart.*[9] **2COR 3:3**

Having received *a new heart of flesh with His law written on it*[9] (Ez 36:26, Jer 31:33), our new path to holiness and *good works*[2a] is through *the law of the Spirit of life in Christ Jesus*[2] (Rom 8:1-2), not by *attempting to keep the law*[18a] *written on tablets of stone*[24] (2Cor 3:3, *The Finished Work of Christ;* Chapter 4).

The New Testament is full of examples and warnings about becoming *enslaved*[24] again by succumbing to the temptation of the flesh *to perfect itself by works and self-effort.*[18a] In no uncertain terms, Paul admonishes in Galatians 5:1-4, that anyone who *attempts to be justified by the law has become a debtor*[18a] to fulfill it completely, once again.

> Stand fast therefore in the *liberty*[1] by which Christ has made us free, and do not be entangled again with a *yoke of bondage.*[24] indeed I, Paul, say to you that if you become circumcised, *Christ will profit you nothing.*[18a] And I testify again to every man who becomes circumcised that he is a *debtor*[20] to keep the whole law.[24] *You have become estranged from Christ, you who attempt to be justified by law; you have fallen from grace.*[18a] **GAL 5:1-4**

THE LEARNING YOKE

Now in this beautiful trade of yokes, we are infinitely the benefactors. Jesus invites us, *"Take my yoke upon you..."*[2a] and in the same breath, describes the kind of yoke it is—*a learning yoke*[2a] (Mat 11:28-30 p27).

Jesus' main job was *teacher.*[13] In the synagogues, from mountain tops, out of a boat, in front of multitudes, with intimate groups, His three years of ministry was spent *teaching*[13] and *signs followed*[3] wherever He went.

> **KEY GREEK WORD**
> **4462 RHABBOUNI:**[13] (hrab-bon-ee') My master, my teacher.

His disciples called Him *"Rabboni,"*[13] and they eagerly walked beside Him, gathered at His table, and sat at His feet—*to learn from Him.*[2a]

When He pronounced Matthew 11:28 (p27), He spoke to every generation alive and those to follow, inviting us all to come and *learn yoked to His side,*[2a] just as the privileged twelve were. But how could we all be as advantaged when He was soon to go to the Father?

> And I will pray the Father, and He will give you *another Helper,*[2a] that He may *abide*[2a] with you forever **JHN 14:16**

ANOTHER OF THE SAME KIND

It is the Holy Spirit who is *another Helper of the same kind as Jesus*[2a] (Jhn 14:16). He is our *Paraclete*[2a] and we have been *yoked together*[2a] with Him, and

> **KEY GREEK WORDS**
> **243 ALLOS:**[2a] (al'-los) another of the same kind. Opposite of **2087 HETEROS,** another of a different kind.

He with us. Furthermore, *He abides with us*[2a] in the same way Jesus abided constantly with the twelve—*but forever. He'll never leave us or forsake us*[2] and we can, and should, *cast all our cares onto Him*[1d] (1Jhn 2:27, Heb 13:5-6, 1Pet 5:7).

> But the *anointing*[2a] which you have received from Him *abides in you,*[2] and *you do not need that anyone teach you;*[2a] but as the same anointing teaches you concerning all things, and is true, and is not a lie, and just *as it has taught you, you will abide in Him.*[2a] **1JHN 2:27**
>
> ... For He Himself has said, *"I will never leave you nor forsake you."*[2] So we may boldly say: *"The Lord is my helper;*[2a] I will not fear. What can man do to me?"* **HEB 13:5-6**
>
> ... *casting all your care upon Him,*[1d] for He cares for you. **1PET 5:7**

All who walked beside Jesus and *submitted under His leadership,*[2a] had all of their needs met. Jesus not only connected His followers to God and brought them into *spiritual understanding*[17a] but He gave them *food to eat, provided for their taxes, healed them,*[5a] and *walked with them*[2] every single day.

In the same way, the Holy Spirit *meets all of our needs,*[5a] as we abide in Him by submitting under His teaching yoke. The *abiding place is living under His leadership*[2a] (*Total Saturation in the Spirit-Empowered Life:* Vol 3; Chapter 2) and we have *no need of any other teacher!*[2a]

Our level of *submission to His leadership*[2a] is in direct proportion to how much of the *power of God*[3] is operating in our lives. God has *freely given us all things*[5a] (Rom 8:32). The only limit is what we have placed on this *heavenly partnership,*[2] either knowingly or unknowingly.

> He who *did not spare His own Son,*[1] but delivered Him up for us all, how shall He not with Him also *freely give us all things?*[5a] **ROM 8:32**

🦶 *This* is the whole context of *New Covenant life*[1d]—being yoked together *under the leadership and teaching anointing of the Holy Spirit*[2a] and the Word of God, and this is how we are proven to be *sons of God*[15] (Phl 4:19, 1Jhn 2:27 p29, Rom 8:14).

> And my God shall *supply all your need*[5a] according to His riches in *glory*[3] by *Christ Jesus.*[1] **PHL 4:19**
>
> For as many as are *led by the Spirit*[2a] of God, these are *sons of God.*[15] **ROM 8:14**

💧 So let's think on this for a moment:

The Holy Spirit, the *creative power of the Godhead, the doer of the Word, the glory of God, the resurrection power,*[3] Himself, is who we are *yoked together with.*[2a] That's an uneven yoke, but in the best possible way we could imagine! What else do we need? *Nothing!*

YOKED TO ONE OR THE OTHER

Every person on the face of the planet is yoked to something. Even after we have been redeemed by the blood of Christ and sealed with the Holy Spirit, we are either *yoked to the law*[24] *and the world,*[27] or *to the Holy Spirit*[2a] *and grace,*[5] and it can change in any given circumstance. Not only must His yoke be purposefully accepted, it must be consciously submitted to, moment by moment, and this is a *learned spiritual skill.*[16]

So this begs the question; who, or what, are we yoked to? Whose teaching are we submitted under? Who is leading us and guiding us? Are we *leading ourselves*[18a] using *natural reasoning*[17b] and information from our *five senses?*[17b] Are we being influenced by the *world's wisdom?*[27]

The gulf between *natural*[10c] and *spiritual truth*[10] is the difference between natural and supernatural fruit. Our faith can be in the *wisdom of men*[27] or the *power of God*[3] (1Cor 2:5 p32). But without the Holy Spirit, no one can even *see or perceive*[10] the things of God at all. It's obvious where we should *surrender*[2a] ourselves (Jhn 14:16-18, 1Cor 2:9 p32).

> And I will pray the Father, and He will give you another Helper, that He may abide with you forever—the Spirit of truth, *whom the world cannot receive, because it neither sees Him nor knows Him;*[20] but *you know Him, for He dwells with you and will be in you.*[2] I will not leave you orphans; I will come to you. **JHN 14:16-18**

In Christ, we have been *yoked together forever with the Paraclete,*[2a] but just like the disciples had free reign to stay by Jesus' side or leave, we do as well.

With our *willing submission,*[2a] and eager desire to continually focus our attention on Him, our loving Paraclete is fully able to do

However, when He, the Spirit of truth, has come, He will **guide you into all truth;**[2a] for He will not speak on His own authority, but **whatever He hears He will speak; and He will tell you things to come.**[4] He will glorify Me, for He will take of what is Mine and declare it to you. All things that the Father has are Mine. Therefore I said that He will take of Mine and declare it to you. JHN 16:13-15

1 CORINTHIANS 2

1 And I, brethren, when I came to you, did not come with excellence of speech or of wisdom declaring to you the testimony of God. **2** For I determined not to know anything among you except Jesus Christ and Him crucified. **3** I was with you in weakness, in fear, and in much trembling. **4** And my speech and my preaching were not with **persuasive words of human wisdom,**[10c] but in demonstration of the Spirit and of power, **5** that your faith should not be in the **wisdom of men**[27] but in the **power of God.**[3]

6 However, we speak **wisdom**[10] among those who are mature, yet not the **wisdom of this age, nor of the rulers of this age,**[27] who are coming to nothing. **7** But we speak the **wisdom of God in a mystery,**[10] the hidden wisdom which God ordained before the ages for our glory, **8** which none of the rulers of this age knew; for had they known, they would not have crucified the Lord of glory.

9 But as it is written: **"Eye has not seen, nor ear heard,**[20] nor have entered into the heart of man the things which God has prepared for those who love Him."

10 But God has **revealed**[10] them to us through His Spirit. For the Spirit searches all things, yes, **the deep things of God.**[10] **11** For what man knows the things of a man except the spirit of the man which is in him? Even so no one **knows the things of God**[10] except the Spirit of God. **12** Now **we have received, not the spirit of the world, but the Spirit who is from God,**[2] that we might **know**[10] the things that have been freely given to us by God.

13 These things we also speak, not in words which **man's wisdom teaches**[10c] but which the **Holy Spirit teaches,**[2a] **comparing spiritual things with spiritual.**[10] **14** But the **natural man**[17b] does not receive the things of the Spirit of God, for they are foolishness to him; nor can he know them, because they are **spiritually discerned.**[17a] **15** But he who is spiritual judges all things, yet he himself is rightly judged by no one. **16** For "who has known the mind of the Lord that he may instruct Him?" But we have **the mind of Christ.**[17a]

His job; *lead us and guide us into all truth*[2a] (Jhn 16:13-15), always *revealing*[10] the *Finished Work of Christ*[1] in every circumstance and empowering us to *walk in it.*[12]

He will continually *reveal the mysteries of God*[10] to us to the point that we can boldly say we have *the mind of Christ*[17a] and *we know all things,*[10] even things to come (1Cor 2:11,12,16)!

THREE
THE MASTER'S COMMAND

I t was Resurrection day—the day the tomb was found empty (Jhn 20:19-22). Behind the closed doors of unfathomable grief, agonizing guilt, bewildering confusion and darkening fear; amongst it all, *there He stood.* They had all witnessed the miracles, but none like this:

1. He showed the marks in His hands and side, giving proof that the wages of sin had been fully paid and the *New Covenant*[1d] had been written in His blood. This *evidence of His resurrection,*[14] proved the Father had accepted His sacrifice, and therefore, *declared our eternal justification*[8] (Rom 4:24-25).

2. He declared *peace with the Father.*[1] The enmity that had separated us since Adam, the middle wall of separation, had now been broken down (Eph 2:14-18).

Then, the same day at evening, being the first day of the week, when the doors were shut where the disciples were assembled, for fear of the Jews, Jesus came and stood in the midst, and said to them, *"Peace be with you."*[1] When He had said this, He showed them His hands and His side. Then the disciples were glad when they saw the Lord. So Jesus said to them again, *"Peace to you!*[1] As the Father has sent Me, I also send you." And when He had said this, *He breathed on them,*[1g] and said to them, *"Receive the Holy Spirit.*[2] JHN 20:19-22

... It shall be imputed to us who believe in Him *who raised up Jesus our Lord from the dead,*[14] who was delivered up because of our offenses, and was *raised because of our justification.*[8] ROM 4:24-25

For *He Himself is our peace,*[1] who has made both one, and has *broken down the middle wall of separation,*[20] having *abolished in His flesh the enmity,*[20] that is, *the law of commandments contained in ordinances,*[24] so as to create in Himself one new man from the two, thus making peace, and that He might reconcile them both to God in one body through the cross, *thereby putting to death the enmity.*[20] And He came and preached *peace*[1] to you who were afar off and to those who were near. For through Him we both have access by one Spirit to the Father. EPH 2:14-18

3. He re-enacted the moment God **breathed life into**[19] Adam (Gen 2:7) —as **He breathed into them**[19] (not on them) saying "Receive the Holy Spirit," He released the **new birth**[19] and they were **filled with the Spirit of God.**[2]

And the Lord God formed man of the dust of the ground, and **breathed into his nostrils**[19] the breath of life; and man became a living soul. **GEN 2:7**

KEY GREEK WORD

1720 EMPHUSAÓ:[19] (em-foo-sah'-o) to breathe **into** or upon † From **1722 EN,** *in* and **5448 PHYSAŌ,** *breathe (blow) in,* inflate.

KEY HEBREW WORD

5301 NAPHACH:[19] (naw-fakh') to breathe, blow.

Now that Jesus was resurrected, **the Holy Spirit could indwell us,**[2] and this was the transcendent moment **He breathed**[19] **the New Creation**[9] into existence! This is the same new birth and automatic **infilling of the Holy Spirit**[2] that happens when anybody receives Christ—they are **born again of incorruptible seed**[9] and inhabited by the presence of God (1Pet 1:23).

having been **born again, not of corruptible seed but incorruptible,**[9] through the word of God which lives and abides forever, **1PET 1:23**

until the day in which He was taken up, after He through the Holy Spirit had given commandments to the apostles whom He had chosen, to whom **He also presented Himself alive after His suffering by many infallible proofs, being seen by them during forty days**[14] and speaking of the things pertaining to the kingdom of God. **ACTS 1:2-3**

HIS LAST COMMAND

Fast forward to Acts 1:2-3, which tells us that **He walked with them for 40 days, infallibly proving Himself to be alive,**[14] and teaching about the kingdom of God.

Now, it was Ascension day and there was one last **command**[3a] of such significance that it was the *very last thing* He left them with before He ascended. These next moments contained **one of His most important directives, the final deposits of instruction**[3a] and understanding before departing to be with the Father.

† Helps Word-Studies

4. He commanded them[3a]
not to depart from Jerusalem, but to wait for the Promise of the Father, the **Baptism of the Holy Spirit**[3a] (Acts 1:4-5). By this, the Holy Spirit would **come upon**[3a] them and empower them to be **witnesses**[13] **of His death and resurrection**[14] "to the end of the earth." (Acts 1:8)

And being assembled together with them, **He commanded them**[3a] not to depart from Jerusalem, but to wait for the Promise of the Father, "which," He said, "you have heard from Me; for John truly baptized with water, but you shall be **baptized with the Holy Spirit**[3a] not many days from now." **ACTS 1:4-5**

But you shall receive power when the Holy Spirit has come upon you; and **you shall be witnesses to Me**[13] in Jerusalem, and in all Judea and Samaria, and to the end of the earth." **ACTS 1:8**

So He released the **infilling**[2] of the Holy Spirit when **He breathed into them**[19] in John 20:21-23. Now, 40 days later, He was commanding them to wait for the Baptism of the Holy Spirit, **the Promise of the Father upon them.**[3a]

TWO APPLICATIONS

The **infilling**[2] of John 20:21-23 and the **enduing upon**[3a] of Luke 24:49 are two different applications of the Holy Spirit. Both are essential for us to walk in the full measure of our redemption. Together, they **seal us with His presence,**[2] and **clothe us with His power**[3a] (Acts 1:8).

Behold, I send the Promise of My Father **upon you;**[3a] but tarry in the city of Jerusalem until you are **endued with power**[3a] from on high." **LK 24:49**

KEY GREEK WORD

1746 ENDUO:[3a] (en-doo'-o) To clothe or be clothed with (in the sense of sinking into a garment).

The infilling of the Holy Spirit[2] is an automatic result of being washed by the blood and proceeds from the **new birth.**[19]

The enduing upon, or the Baptism of the Holy Spirit,[3a] is something we must actively receive—*and it's not a suggestion!*

The *command*[3a] that Jesus gave in His last moments on earth is directed at all of us still today—receive *the Promise of the Father*[3a] and the divine *power*[3] that comes with Him.

THE BAPTISM OF THE HOLY SPIRIT

As unmistakably as the *breath of God*[19] goes *inside us,*[2] the *Baptism of the Holy Spirit*[3a] *completes us* (explained p45) on the outside and results in *power.*[3]

Acts 2:2 describes the sound from heaven that was like a mighty rushing wind that filled the whole house. They were sitting *in* the house as it was filled with the Holy Spirit (Chapter 8), and just like the *picture of water Baptism,*[19] they were *immersed in the glory,*[3a] completely saturated *on the outside.*[3a]

> **1** When the Day of Pentecost had fully come, they were all with one accord in one place. **2** And suddenly there came a sound from heaven, as of a rushing mighty wind, and it filled the whole house where they were sitting. **3** Then there appeared to them divided tongues, as of fire, and one sat *upon*[3a] each of them. **4** And they were all *filled*[3a] with the Holy Spirit and began to speak with other tongues, as the Spirit gave them utterance. **ACTS 2:1-4**

THE PICTURE OF THE ARK OF THE COVENANT

With both applications of the Holy Spirit, we are the substance of the picture of the Ark of the Covenant. In the Old Testament, this hallowed vessel carried the presence of the living God, but it was merely the shadow and type of *us,* the true vessel and temple of the Lord.

The ark was made of acacia wood and covered on the *inside*[2] and *outside*[3a] with pure gold. The acacia wood represents us, the flawed natural vessel. The gold represents the Holy Spirit—we are filled on the *inside*[2] and saturated on the *outside*[3a] with the *glory of God.*[3] The picture is only complete in us with *both* applications of the Holy Spirit, and will be finalized at *our resurrection*[14]—it will be all gold!

THE GREATEST AREA OF CONTENTION

The Baptism of the Holy Spirit[3a] and *accompanying sign of tongues*[3b] (Mk 16:17) is one of the most misunderstood and disputed points of the Bible. It's not surprising, since according to Acts

> And these signs will follow those who believe: In My name they will cast out demons; *they will speak in new tongues;*[3b] **MK 16:17**

1:4-5 and 8 (p36), this is how the church is sent out into the world to *continue the present-day ministry of Christ;*[13] to free the captives, to set at liberty those who are oppressed of the devil (Lk 4:18-19, Acts 10:38), and to do the *works*[3] He did and even greater (Jhn 14:11-14). The enemy's reign over the world and control over the sons of disobedience is severely threatened by a church that truly comprehends and operates in its *power*[3] and *authority.*[15]

> *"The Spirit of the Lord is upon Me, because He has anointed*[3] Me to preach the gospel to the poor; He has sent Me to heal the brokenhearted, to proclaim liberty to the captives and recovery of sight to the blind, to set at liberty those who are oppressed; To proclaim the acceptable year of the Lord." **LK 4:18-19**
>
> *how God anointed Jesus of Nazareth with the Holy Spirit and with power,*[3] who went about doing good and healing all who were oppressed by the devil, for God was with Him. **ACTS 10:38**
>
> Believe Me that I am in the Father and the Father in Me, or else believe Me for the sake of the works themselves. "Most assuredly, I say to you, *he who believes*[7] *in Me, the works*[3] *that I do he will do also;* and *greater works*[3] than these he will do, because I go to My Father. And whatever you ask in My name, that I will do, that the Father may be glorified in the Son. If you ask anything in My name, I will do it. **JHN 14:11-14**

But *without the Baptism of the Holy Spirit*[3a] and *accompanying sign of tongues,*[3b] we are essentially operating in the enemy's terrain without the powerful tactical equipment and guidance system issued by our *commanding officer.*[3a]

How can we give any more room to the enemy and keep arguing this point? In Luke 4:18-19, Jesus was essentially saying, *"I have an anointing*[2a] *and this is what it does..."*[3] Acts 10:38 describes the same *power*[3] and purpose. Now through the Baptism of the Holy Spirit, we've been given the same *anointing*[2a] for the same objective (1Jhn 2:27, Acts 1:8 p36)—to *preach the gospel,*[13] not in word only, *but in demonstration of the Spirit*[2a] *and power*[3] (1Th 1:5, 1Cor 2:4).

BORN FILLED

Jesus had the *infilling*[2] of the Holy Spirit from birth. He was not born of the *Adamic seed,*[20] but of the divine seed that Mary received *when the Holy Spirit overshadowed her*[3a] (Lk 1:34-35, Chapter 5). Jesus didn't have the same *corrupted nature*[20] that we had and, as a man, this is how He was different to us.

> But the *anointing*[2a] which you have received from Him *abides in you,*[2a] ... **1JHN 2:27**
>
> For our gospel did not come to you in word only, but also *in power,*[3] *and in the Holy Spirit*[2a] and in much assurance, as you know what kind of men we were among you for your sake. **1TH 1:5**
>
> And my speech and my preaching were not with *persuasive words of human wisdom,*[10c] but in *demonstration of the Spirit*[2a] *and of power,*[3] **1COR 2:4**
>
> Then Mary said to the angel, "How can this be, since I do not know a man?" And the angel answered and said to her, *"The Holy Spirit will come upon you, and the power of the Highest will overshadow you;*[3a] therefore, also, that Holy One who is to be born will be called the Son of God. **LK 1:34-35**
>
> For as by *one man's disobedience*[23] many were *made sinners,*[20] so also by *one Man's obedience*[1] many will be *made righteous.*[8] **ROM 5:19**

To clarify an important distinction; *committing sins*[20a] doesn't make us *sinners,*[20] rather sinners automatically sin because of the *sin nature*[20] we are born with (Rom 5:19). This is why sin had dominion over us before we received the *New Creation heart,*[9] and why everyone needs the Savior to be freed from this *corruption.*[20] (*The Finished Work of Christ;* Chapter 3).

> For we do not have a High Priest who cannot sympathize with our weaknesses, but was in all points tempted as we are, *yet without sin.*[20] **HEB 4:15**

In Hebrews 4:15 where it says, Jesus was tempted as we are, *yet without sin,*[20] it means He didn't sin because He was *without the sin nature*[20] from which sins are the outworking. Otherwise, sin would've existed in Him and He couldn't have qualified to be our *spotless lamb.*[1b]

So Jesus had the *infilling of the Holy Spirit²* since birth, but now everything was about to change.

THE PIVOTAL MOMENT HIS MIRACLE MINISTRY BEGAN

> What is man that You are mindful of him, and the son of man that You visit him? For You have made him a little lower than the angels, and You have **crowned him with glory and honor.**³ᵃ **PS 8:4-5**
>
> When all the people were baptized, it came to pass that Jesus also was baptized; and while He prayed, the heaven was opened. And **the Holy Spirit descended in bodily form like a dove upon Him,** and a voice came from heaven which said, **"You are My beloved Son; in You I am well pleased."** Now Jesus Himself **began His ministry at about thirty years of age,...**³ **LK 3:21-23**

Jesus received the *enduing upon, the Baptism of the Holy Spirit,*³ᵃ at the same time of His water Baptism. It wasn't until this moment when Jesus was *"clothed with glory and honor"* ³ᵃ that *His miracle ministry began*³ (Ps 8:4-5, Lk 3:21-23). Let's understand through some 📖 shadows and types.

Clothed With Glory and Honor

*Glory,*³ an expression of the Holy Spirit (Chapter 4), is always accompanied by the DUNAMIS, *miracle-working power of God.*³ Wherever the glory is, there is power.

*Honor*³ᶠ is the endorsement and backing of God and is equivalent to EXOUSIA *authority.*¹⁵ Looking at this definition, we're authorized to act to the extent of our faith. In other words, since faith arises from hearing (p22), what we hear

KEY GREEK WORDS

1411 DUNAMIS:³ (doo'-nam-is) Miraculous power, might, strength. "Power through God's ability"

1849 EXOUSIA:¹⁵ (ex-oo-see'-ah) Power to act, authority. † Conferred power, *delegated empowerment,*³ operating in a designated jurisdiction. *Refers to the authority God gives to His saints, authorizing them to act to the extent they are guided by faith (His revealed Word).*

is what we are authorized to complete. Now, sent in the *delegated authority*¹⁵ of the Father, He *honors*³ᶠ and backs us with His *power.*³

Before the fall, *Adam was clothed with glory and honor*[3a] (Ps 8:4-5). This *"clothing"* was far more than something that caused him to be naked and not ashamed. It was a garment of *power*[3] and *authority*[15] bestowed on Him by the Father—just like Joseph's coat, which is another *type.*[19]

🦶 So in Luke 3:21-23, when the Holy Spirit descended *upon*[3a] Jesus like a dove, He was *overshadowed*[3a] (Chapter 5) with power from on high. In the same moment, He received the *endorsement*[15] of the Father, "... my beloved Son in whom I am well pleased." Jesus was now *fully clothed with glory and honor,*[3a] *dunamis power*[3] and *exousia authority.*[15] He became the *authorized*[15] and *empowered*[3] Son.

> Then Jesus answered and said to them, "Most assuredly, I say to you, the Son can do nothing of Himself, but what He sees the Father do; for *whatever He does, the Son also does in like manner.*[2a] JHN 5:19

In the same way the Son of God *"could do nothing of Himself"* (Jhn 5:19) and needed the *glory of God,*[3] the *enduing-upon of the Holy Spirit,*[3a] to manifest the *miracle-working power*[3] in the earth, so do we. It's the very same *garment*[3a] that we have been commanded to be clothed with (Lk 24:49 p36). In the same way as Jesus, we live the *Spirit-empowered life*[3] as *authorized,*[15] *empowered*[3] *sons of God.*[15]

LESSON 8

DID JESUS PRAY IN TONGUES?

Many ask why we don't see evidence in Scripture of Jesus praying in tongues. As the Son of God, He already had everything that the gift of tongues provides for the New Testament believer.

Tongues[3b] brings us *revelation*[10] and clarity *to know the voice of the Father.*[4] Whereas, Jesus was *indwelt by the Holy Spirit*[2] since birth and was about *doing His Father's business from a very early age*[2a] (Lk 2:49).

> And He said to them, "Why did you seek Me? Did you not know that *I must be about My Father's business?"*[2a] LK 2:49

Since there was no hindrance from *corruption*[20] to their fellowship (p39), Jesus was by nature *willing and able to submit*[2a] to the Father, *hearing*[4] and being *obedient*[2a] to only do what He heard the Father say. Then at His Baptism, He received the *full power*[3a] to carry out the work of His ministry.

In contrast, through our *prayer language*[3a] we *choose to submit to His leadership.*[2a] The Spirit helps us with our weaknesses and we go from *not knowing*[10b] what to pray, *to knowing all things*[10] (Rom 8:26-28, 1Jhn 2:20). Our prayer language helps us to perceive and submit to *spiritual relationship,*[2a] but Jesus already had this from birth.

> Likewise the Spirit also helps in our weaknesses. For *we do not know*[10b] what we should pray for as we ought, but the Spirit Himself makes intercession for us with groanings which cannot be uttered. Now He who searches the hearts knows what the mind of the Spirit is, because He makes intercession for the saints according to the will of God. *And we know*[10] that all things work together for good to those who love God, to those who are the called according to His purpose. **ROM 8:26-28**
>
> But you have an anointing from the Holy One, and *you know all things.*[10] **1JHN 2:20**

ETERNAL SALVATION WITHOUT EMPOWERMENT

> Now when the apostles who were at Jerusalem heard that Samaria had received the word of God, they sent Peter and John to them, who, when they had come down, prayed for them that they might receive the Holy Spirit. For as yet He had *fallen upon*[3a] none of them. They had only been *baptized in the name of the Lord Jesus.*[1h] Then they laid hands on them, and *they received the Holy Spirit.*[3a] **ACTS 8:14-17**

It's possible, even common in the church, to have been *sealed with the Holy Spirit*[2] and have eternal life by the forgiveness of sins, but not receive the *fullness*[3a] of what he intended (see p45). In fact it is described here in Acts 8:14-17.

Samaria received the gospel and had been *baptized in the name of the Lord Jesus.*[1h] Clearly they were believers who had received the *automatic infilling of the Holy Spirit*[2] at their salvation. But the Holy Spirit had not yet *fallen upon*[3a] them.

3: THE MASTER'S COMMAND

> ... And finding some disciples he said to them, "Did you receive the Holy Spirit when you believed?" So they said to him, "We have not so much as heard whether there is a Holy Spirit." And he said to them, "into what then were you baptized?" So they said, "into John's Baptism." Then Paul said, "John indeed baptized with a Baptism of repentance, saying to the people that they should believe on Him who would come after him, that is, on Christ Jesus." When they heard this, they were baptized in the name of the Lord Jesus. And **when Paul had laid hands on them, the Holy Spirit came upon them,**[3a] and they **spoke with tongues**[3b] **and prophesied.**[4a] **ACTS 19:1-6**

Likewise in Acts 19:1-6, the disciples who were **baptized**[1h] into John's Baptism were clearly believers of Jesus, because that's what John preached. As soon as Paul laid hands on them, **they spoke with tongues**[3b] **and prophesied**[4a]—a result of Holy Spirit **empowerment**[3] (Chapter 6).

It's interesting to note that in Acts 10:44, and 46-48, they received the **Holy Spirit**[3a] upon the word that Peter preached, *before water Baptism.*[1h] Also, this scripture proves **the evidence of having received the Baptism of the Holy Spirit**[3a] **is speaking in tongues.**[3b] How do we know this? Verse 44 says the **Holy Spirit fell upon them,**[3a] then in verse 46 it says they knew that because they **heard them speak in tongues.**[3b]

> **44** While Peter was still speaking these words, the **Holy Spirit fell upon**[3a] all those who heard the word. ... **46** **For they heard them** **speak with tongues**[3b] and magnify God. Then Peter answered, **47** "Can anyone forbid water, that these should not be baptized who have received the Holy Spirit just as we have?" **48** And he commanded them to be **baptized in the name of the Lord.**[1h] **ACTS 10:44, 46-48**

🜄 Just like these believers could not remain without, how can we live with anything less than the what He **commanded**[3a] us to receive? How could we think we could be fully effective to go into all the world and preach the gospel and **demonstrate His power**[3] without His Baptism **upon us**[3a] (Acts 1:8 p36). How can we **clearly hear**[4] and do what the Father says in every moment? How could we even be successful in our own lives against the constant onslaught in our mind of the **wicked one**[21a] without His **supernatural empowerment?**[3]

43

The *Baptism of the Holy Spirit*[3a] is not a suggestion, *it's a command.*[3a] This is, or rather *He is,* the *completion*[3a] of the *New Creation man*[9] (p45 & Chapter 6). *His abiding presence*[2] and *power*[3] is the difference between the Old Testament saint and the New Testament saint. To hear from God, they had to go to the prophet, priest, or king. *Now we have the ability to intimately perceive, and be led by His prophetic voice.*[4] He speaks to every one of us directly, from the least, to the greatest (Jer 31:34, Isa 28:11).

> For *with stammering lips and another tongue*[3b] He will *speak to this people,*[4]... ISA 28:11

> No more shall every man teach his neighbor, and every man his brother, saying, '*Know* (YADA/GINÓSKÓ) the LORD,' for they all shall *know* (YADA/EIDÓ) Me, from the least of them to the greatest of them, says the LORD. For I will forgive their iniquity, and their sin I will remember no more." JER 31:34

KEY HEBREW WORD

3045 YADA: (yaw-dah') To know, perceive, understand, acknowledge.

CORRESPONDING GREEK WORD

1097 GINÓSKÓ: (ghin-oce'-ko)to come to know fully, recognize, perceive. Implies a deep, personal, and relational knowledge, such as the intimate relationship between a husband and wife, and the covenant relationship between God and His people. Sexual intimacy (Lk 1:34).

1492 EIDÓ (OIDA): (i'-do) be aware, behold, perceive. † A gateway to grasp spiritual truth. * *The ability to know the prophetic voice, able to be led.*

THE SIGN OF TONGUES

Scripture is clear every New Testament saint in the early church received the *Baptism of the Holy Spirit*[3a] and it was *evidenced by speaking in tongues*[3b] (Acts 10:44,46-48 p43).

In Mark 16:17, Jesus himself gives another undeniable description of *every New Testament believer*[7] as those who will *speak with tongues.*[3b]

> "And these *signs*[3] will accompany those who *believe:*[7] in my name they will cast out demons; they will *speak in new tongues;...*"[3b] MK 16:17 ESV

* Thayer's Greek Lexicon

Paul, the greatest *revelator*[10] of the New Testament said *"I thank God I speak with tongues*[3b] *more than you all"* (1Cor 14:18). He received the *wisdom*[10] by which he penned three quarters of the New Testament from no man, but by *revelation*[10] (Gal 1:12).

> I thank my God *I speak with tongues*[3a] more than you all; **1COR 14:18**
>
> For I neither received it from man, nor was I taught it, but *it came through the revelation of Jesus Christ.*[10] **GAL 1:12**

We too, *do only what the Father says*[4] by *revelation*[10] in *relationship with the Holy Spirit*[2] and the *Word of God.*[1c] The rock the church is built upon is the *rock of revelation*[10] (Mat 16:17-18), and it is how *true Biblical faith arises.*[7] Following Paul's example, *"stammering lips," or praying in tongues*[3b] (Isa 28:11), is the way we develop our sensitivity to *spiritually perceive*[4] what He's saying right now. Clearly *hearing,*[4] we receive *revelation,*[10] and *walk*[12] in the *faith*[7] that arises from it (Rom 10:17). *Edification,*[13a] or being *built*[13a] *on the rock*[10] is the result (Jd 1:20, Chapter 6, *Total Saturation in the Spirit-Empowered Life:* Vol 2; Chapters 1 & 2).

> Jesus answered and said to him, "Blessed are you, Simon Bar-Jonah, for flesh and blood has not *revealed*[10] this to you, but My Father who is in heaven. And I also say to you that you are Peter, and *on this rock*[10] *I will build My church,*[13a] and the gates of Hades shall not prevail against it. **MAT 16:17-18**

> So then *faith comes*[7] by *(spiritually perceiving) hearing,*[4] and hearing by the **(RHÉMA)** *word*[4] of God. **ROM 10:17**
>
> But you, beloved, *building yourselves up*[13a] on your most holy faith, *praying in the Holy Spirit,*[3b] **JD 1:20**
>
> **KEY GREEK WORDS**
>
> **189 AKOÉ:**[4] (ak-o-ay') hearing. † Inner (spiritual) hearing, *discerning God's voice.*

THE COMPLETION OF THE NEW CREATION MAN

Paul's instruction to *"be filled with the Spirit"*[3a] in Ephesians 5:18 was actually a command, just like Jesus' command in Acts 1:4-5 (p36). The Greek word, **4137 PLÉROÓ**,[3a] would be better translated as *"be completed."*[3a] This describes the completing work of the *Baptism of the Holy Spirit.*[3a]

> And do not be drunk with wine, in which is dissipation; but *be filled*[3a] with the Spirit,
> **EPH 5:18**
>
> ## KEY GREEK WORDS
>
> **4137 PLÉROÓ:**[3a] (play-ro'-o) to make full, *to complete.* Fill to individual capacity, or *bring something to completion.*

🔑 It's written in the present tense, imperative mood and active voice, so his instructions might better be translated as, *"I command you, be constantly being completed by the Holy Spirit."*[3a] He's essentially saying we must do it. How? Through purposefully using our *prayer language*[3b] while meditating on the Word, we are *continually completed*[3a] or matured in *revelation understanding*[10] of the Finished Work of Christ. This is how we *submit under the leadership anointing of the Holy Spirit*[2a] and in doing so, we'll operate in the full function of *the New Creation man,*[9] able to receive all the *salvation provision*[5a] of God by *faith.*[7]

In this new *"completed"*[3a] state we access the *large down payment*[2] of *our future resurrection,*[14] which is more than sufficient to receive the *supernatural provision*[5a] we need.

<u>This</u> is the stark contrast between the Old Testament and New Testament saint (Eph 1:13-14).

> in Him you also trusted, after you heard the word of truth, the gospel of your salvation; in whom also, having believed, you were *sealed with the Holy Spirit*[2] of promise, who is the *guarantee*[2] of our inheritance until the *redemption of the purchased possession,*[14] to the praise of His glory.
> **EPH 1:13-14**
>
> ## KEY GREEK WORD
>
> **728 ARRABÓN:**[2] (ar-hrab-ohn') an earnest deposit, a large part of the payment given in advance as a security that the whole will be paid afterwards, guarantees the balance.

FUNCTIONING AS EMPOWERED SONS

🜕 Receiving and *continually submitting to the Holy Spirit*[2a] is so vitally important that Jesus not only commanded them, and us, but this is *the very reason*[30] He hung on the cursed tree (Gal 3:13-14).

Of course, saving us from eternal condemnation is first, but it's not all. Our salvation is not just for us. It's *so that*[30] we could receive *the blessing of Abraham*[8] (eternal justification by faith), *so that*[30] we qualify to receive *the promise of the Father*[3a] and walk in the same divine power He did for the same purpose of *reaching the world with the gospel*[13] (Acts 1:8 p36).

Christ has redeemed us from the curse of the law, having become a curse for us (for it is written, "Cursed is everyone who hangs on a tree"), *that*[30] *the blessing of Abraham*[8] might come upon the Gentiles in Christ Jesus, *that*[30] we might receive *the promise of the Spirit*[3a] through faith. **GAL 3:13-14**

KEY GREEK WORD

2443 HINA:[30] (hin'-ah) in order that, that, *so that.*

Therefore, having been justified by faith, *we have peace with God*[1] through our Lord Jesus Christ, through whom also we have *access by faith*[7] into this *grace*[5] in which we *stand,*[12] and rejoice in *hope*[31] of the *glory of God.*[3] **ROM 5:1-2**

Let us therefore come boldly to the throne of grace, that we may obtain mercy and find *grace to help in time of need.*[5] **HEB 4:16**

... *In mighty signs and wonders,*[3] by the power of the Spirit of God, so that from Jerusalem and round about to Illyricum *I have fully preached*[13] the *gospel of Christ.*[1] **ROM 15:19**

KEY GREEK WORD

1680 ELPIS:[31] (el-pece') Hope. † *Expectation of what is sure (certain).*

We have access, or entrance, into *grace*[5] by *faith*[7] (Rom 5:1-2). Grace is His ability, His *empowerment,*[3] and it must be received by faith. So as we go out into the world, from our position of *peace with God,*[1] we can, *and must,* place a *sure expectation*[31] on the *glory of God*[3] to show up *in time of need*[5] (Heb 4:16), in *demonstration of His power.*[3] This is how we *fully preach*[13] the gospel,*[1] not in word only, but in *power*[3] (Rom 15:19).

† Helps Word-Studies

This critically underestimated gift of God, **the Baptism of the Holy Spirit is the completion**[3a] of the New Testament saint. We are simply not operating in the New Covenant if we're not functioning **under the glory.**[3a] We must do everything by the Holy Spirit, or we are merely an Old Testament saint on this side of the

> "Most assuredly, I say to you, **he who believes in Me,**[7] the **works that I do he will do also;**[3] and greater works than these he will do, because I go to My Father. And whatever you ask in My name, that I will do, that the Father may be glorified in the Son. If you ask anything in My name, I will do it. **JHN 14:12-14**

Cross. Through the Baptism of the Holy Spirit, Jesus made a way for us to function in the **same power**[3] and **anointing**[2a] (Jhn 14:12-14), to **walk as He did**[12] **in authorized,**[15] **empowered**[3] **sonship,**[15] to carry on His calling as **witnesses to the end of earth.**[13]

FOUR

THE GLORY

Decades in the making, Solomon's grand scale celebration of the completion of the temple in Jerusalem, and its solemn dedication, was one of the most exuberant and reverential occasions in Biblical history.

The **blood was shed first,**[1] and the **mercy**[6] of God was poured out. Then God endorsed this long-awaited moment by accepting the sacrifice and thoroughly consuming it with His holy fire. Only then could **God's glory, His presence, fill the house.**[3]

The power of His presence was so intense, the glory cloud so thick, that the priests could not even stand to minister (2Chr 7:1-3, 5:14)!

While the glory filling the temple is the Old Covenant shadow and type, **the outpouring of the Holy Spirit upon all flesh at Pentecost**[3a] in the New Covenant is the substance (Joel 2:28, Chapters 3 & 6).

When Solomon had finished praying, fire came down from heaven and consumed the burnt offering and the sacrifices; and **the glory of the LORD filled the temple.**[3] And **the priests could not enter the house of the LORD, because the glory of the LORD had filled the LORD's house.**[3] When all the children of Israel saw how the fire came down, and the glory of the LORD on the temple, they bowed their faces to the ground on the pavement, and worshiped and praised the LORD, saying: "For He is good, for His mercy endures forever." **2CHR 7:1-3**

So that **the priests could not stand to minister by reason of the cloud: for the glory of the LORD had filled the house of God.**[3] **2CHR 5:14 KJV**

"And it shall come to pass afterward that I will **pour out My Spirit on all flesh;**[3a] your sons and your daughters shall prophesy, your old men shall dream dreams, your young men shall see visions. **JOEL 2:28**

THE LIVING TEMPLE FILLED WITH THE GLORY

The glory filling the body of Christ,[3a] both individually and corporately, is the completed plan of the Old Testament picture. Now *we* are the *temple of the living God*[2] (1Cor 3:16)!

Having been washed by the blood of Christ, recipients of His mercy, we receive *eternal justification*[8] and we have *peace with God the Father*[1] (Rom 5:1). Therefore, we *qualify* to be filled, or rather *completed*[3a] by His Holy Spirit (Gal 3:13-14, Chapter 3). Through *relationship, submitting to His leadership*[2a] we will be utterly transformed by the *glory*[3] from the inside-out.

WHAT IS THE GLORY?

❶ Even though we know Adam was *clothed in the glory*[3a] (Psalm 8:5), the actual first mention of the glory isn't until Exodus 16:6-7.

God is always present but sometimes He wants us to know it by revealing His *tangible, visible power and presence—the glory.*[3] Before the temple in Jerusalem, it was the tabernacle in the wilderness, and the Ark of the Covenant that carried the presence of the Lord. *His glory was visible in the cloud*[3] that led the Israelites by day and *in the fire*[3] that led them by night (Ex 40:34-38).

> Do you not know that *you are the temple of God*[2] and that the Spirit of God dwells in you? **1COR 3:16**
>
> Therefore, having been justified by faith, *we have peace with God*[1] through our Lord Jesus Christ, **ROM 5:1**
>
> Christ has redeemed us from the curse of the law, having become a curse for us (for it is written, "Cursed is everyone who hangs on a tree"), *that*[30] the *blessing of Abraham*[8] might come upon the Gentiles in Christ Jesus, *that*[30] we might receive the *promise of the Spirit*[3a] through faith. **GAL 3:13-14**
>
> For You have made him a little lower than the angels, and *You have crowned him with glory and honor.*[3a] **PS 8:5**
>
> Then Moses and Aaron said to all the children of Israel, "At evening you shall know that the Lord has brought you out of the land of Egypt. And in the morning *you shall see the glory of the Lord;*[3] ..." **EX 16:6-7**

> Then the cloud covered the tabernacle of meeting, and **the glory of the Lord filled the tabernacle.**[3] And Moses was not able to enter the tabernacle of meeting, because **the cloud**[3] rested above it, and the glory of the Lord filled the tabernacle. Whenever the cloud was taken up from above the tabernacle, the children of Israel would go onward in all their journeys. But if the cloud was not taken up, then they did not journey till the day that it was taken up. For **the cloud of the Lord was above the tabernacle by day, and fire was over it by night,**[3] in the <u>sight</u> of all the house of Israel, throughout all their journeys. **EX 40:34-38**
>
> Now **the glory of the Lord**[3] rested on Mount Sinai, and **the cloud**[3] covered it six days. And on the seventh day He called to Moses out of the midst of the cloud. The <u>**sight of the glory of the Lord was like a consuming fire**</u>[3] on the top of the mountain <u>**in the eyes**</u> of the children of Israel. So Moses went into the midst of the cloud and went up into the mountain. And Moses was on the mountain forty days and forty nights. **EX 24:16-18**

The glory[3] was a fearful <u>*sight*</u> resting on top of Mt Sinai and was described as *a consuming fire*[3] as Moses entered the cloud to stand before the presence of God to receive the Ten Commandments (Ex 24:16-18).

THE GLORY IN THE NEW COVENANT

In Romans 6:4-5, we see that Christ was raised from the dead by the *glory of the Father.*[3] Then in Romans 8:11 we see that it was the *Spirit*[3] that raised Jesus from the dead. Conclusively, we can see that not only are the glory and the Holy Spirit one, but also the *resurrection power.*[3] More precisely, the glory and the resurrection power are expressions of the Holy Spirit.

> Therefore we were buried with Him through Baptism into death, that just as **Christ was raised from the dead by the glory of the Father,**[3] even so[29] we also should **walk**[12] in **newness of life.**[9] For if we have been united together in the likeness of His death, certainly we also shall be in the likeness of His resurrection, **ROM 6:4-5**
>
> But if **the Spirit of Him who raised Jesus from the dead**[3] dwells in you, He who raised Christ from the dead will also give life to your mortal bodies through His Spirit who dwells in you. **ROM 8:11**

WALKING IN THE GLORY

Not only does the *resurrection power*[3] transform the heart of stone to the New Creation heart of flesh, *but it forever empowers[3] our walk*[12] (Ez 36:26-27, Jer 31:33 KJV).

In the very same manner[32] that Jesus was *resurrected by the glory,*[3] we should *walk*[12] in *newness of life*[9]—by the *glory,*[3] by the *resurrection power*[3] of the Holy Spirit (Rom 6:4-5 p51). This means *the way*[32] in which we *conduct our everyday life*[12] as New Creation saints should be by supernatural empowerment—by the *outworking of the glory.*[3]

> I will give you a new heart and put a new spirit within you; I will take the heart of stone out of your flesh and give you a heart of flesh. I will put My Spirit within you and *cause you to walk*[12] *in My statutes,*[9] and you will keep My judgments and do them. **EZ 36:26-27 KJV**

> But this shall be the covenant that I will make with the house of Israel; After those days, saith the Lord, I will put my law in their inward parts, and write it in their hearts; and will be their God, and they shall be my people. **JER 31:33 KJV**

KEY GREEK WORDS

3779 HOUTÓ:[29] (hoo'-to) in this way, thus, in this manner.

4043 PERIPATEÓ:[12] (per-ee-pat-eh'-o) to walk. Hebraistically (in an ethical sense): I conduct my life, live.

So the *glory is the supernatural empowerment of the Holy Spirit.*[3] It's the *same resurrection power that rose Christ from the dead.*[3]

> Therefore, having been justified by faith, we have peace with God through our Lord Jesus Christ, through whom also we have *access by faith*[7] into this *grace*[5] in which *we stand,*[13] and rejoice in *hope*[31] of the *glory of God.*[3] **ROM 5:1-2**

KEY GREEK WORD

1680 ELPIS:[31] (el-pece') Expectation, hope. † *Expectation of what is sure (certain).*

It's not only available to us, but God *intends* for us to *walk in it*[12] daily by placing a *sure expectation*[31] on it. When we access *His grace*[5] *by faith,*[7] we access all the *grace provisions*[5a] included in our salvation —healing, provision, protection and favor—through the *glory,*[3] *His abiding Spirit*[2a] (Rom 5:1-2).

† Helps Word-Studies

THE WEIGHT OF THE GLORY

There is another important aspect about understanding the word *"glory,"*[3] throughout the Bible. The definition of the Hebrew word **3519 KABOWD**,[3f] is so vast, but it includes words like honor, abundance, splendor, and wealth. Both the Greek and Hebrew words for *glory*[3f] speak of its weightiness. In the definition of the Greek word **1391 DOXA**,[3f] we see that giving weight, or glory to something is exercising our personal opinion to put value on it. Conversely, we curse a thing when we treat it lightly, consider it insignificant and give it no weight.

KEY HEBREW WORD

3519 KABOWD:[3f] (kaw-bode') glorious. Weight, but only figuratively in a good sense, splendor or copiousness —glorious(ly), glory, honor(able).

KEY GREEK WORDS

1391 DOXA:[3f] (dox'-ah) good opinion, praise, honor, glory, an especially divine quality, the unspoken manifestation of God, splendor. † From **DOKEŌ**, *"exercising personal opinion which determines value."* Corresponds to the OT word, **3519 KABOWD** "to be heavy." Both terms convey God's infinite, intrinsic worth.

7043 QALAL:[3f] (kaw-lal') Accursed, contemptible, insignificant, lightly esteemed, treat with contempt, treated lightly, trivial. (Opposite of **3519 KABOWD** and **1391 DOXA**).

When we give God glory,[3f] we give weight to what He has said by exercising our personal opinion to determine the value of His Word as far greater than anything we see with our natural eyes. In other words, *believing God*[7] is how we give Him glory, honor and praise.

When God gives weight to something, He bears witness to it by bringing his tangible presence and power upon it—a supernatural outpouring of the *glory.*[3]

THE PURPOSE OF THE GLORY

Jesus described the whole plan and purpose of the glory when He said *"The Spirit of the Lord is upon me..."*[3a] The supernatural power of God is given to *preach*[13] *the gospel,*[1] to heal the brokenhearted, to *free*[1] *the*

† Helps Word-Studies

> *"The Spirit of the Lord is upon Me, because He has anointed[2a]* Me
> to *preach[13] the gospel[1]* to the poor; He has *sent[13]* Me to heal the
> brokenhearted, to *proclaim[13] liberty[1]* to the captives and recovery of sight
> to the blind, to *set[13] at liberty[1]* those who are oppressed; to *proclaim[13]*
> the acceptable year of the Lord." **LK 4:18-19**

captives,[20] to *bring recovery of sight[1e] to the blind[20]* etc (Lk 4:18-19).

🜄 Everything to do with Jesus' calling is what is *weighty in God's
eyes.[3f]* In fact, the whole Bible can be summed up as this: God's entire
desire for His creation is displayed in the *greatest expression of His
love—the Finished Work of Christ.[1]* He gave His son so completely
to pay the price of condemnation that was upon us all, so He could
restore us to *personal relationship[2]* with Him for all eternity, and
anoint us[2a] with His glory.[3] He withheld nothing!

LESSON 10

FROM GLORY TO GLORY AND FAITH TO FAITH

Termed the *ministry of death and ministry of condemnation[24]* (2Cor
3:7-9), even so, the *law written on tablets of stone[24]* was glorious. So
much so, that every time Moses returned from being in the presence
of the Lord *his face shone with the glory.[3]* The children of Israel were
so fearful at the sight, Moses had to veil his face (Ex 34:29-30, 33).

> **29** Now it was so, when Moses came down from Mount Sinai (and *the two tablets of the Testimony[24]* were in Moses' hand when he came down from the mountain), that Moses did not know that the skin of his *face shone[3]* while he talked with Him. **30** So when Aaron and all the children of Israel saw Moses, behold, *the skin of his face shone, and they were afraid to come near him.[3]* ... **33** And when Moses had finished speaking with them, *he put a veil on his face.[20]* **EX 34:29-30, 33**

Unable to be near Moses when
the glory was upon him is akin
to all the other instances the
Israelites were unable to stand
in the presence of the glory (e.g.
2Chr 7:1-3, 5:14 p49).

It's important to recognize
occurrences of the glory in the
Old Testament were *outward
visible displays of His power,[3]* as
opposed to *the glory that works*

6 who also made us sufficient as ministers of the new covenant, not of the letter but of the Spirit; for *the letter kills,[24]* but *the Spirit gives life.[19]* **7** But if the *ministry of death, written and engraved on stones,[24] was glorious,[3]* so that the children of Israel could not look steadily at the face of Moses because of the glory of his countenance, which glory was passing away, **8** how will the *ministry of the Spirit[2a]* not be more glorious? **9** For if *the ministry of condemnation[24] had glory,[3]* the ministry of *righteousness[8] exceeds much more in glory.[3]* **10** For even what was made glorious had no glory in this respect, because of the glory that excels. **11** For if *what is passing away[24] was glorious,[3]* what remains is much more glorious. **12** Therefore, since we have such *hope,[31]* we use great boldness of speech— **13** unlike Moses, who put a veil over his face so that the children of Israel could not look steadily at the end of what was passing away. **14** *But their minds were blinded.[20]* For until this day the same veil remains unlifted in the reading of the Old Testament, because *the veil is taken away in Christ.[10]* **15** But even to this day, when Moses is read, a veil lies on their heart. **16** Nevertheless when one turns to the Lord, the veil is taken away. **17** Now the Lord is the Spirit; and *where the Spirit of the Lord is, there is liberty.[1]* **18** But we all, with unveiled face, beholding as in a mirror the glory of the Lord, *are being transformed into the same image from glory to glory,[3]* just as by the Spirit of the Lord. **2COR 3:6-18**

3 But even *if our gospel is veiled, it is veiled to those who are perishing,[20]* **4** whose minds the god of this age has blinded, who do not believe, lest *the light[10] of the gospel of the glory of Christ,[1]* who is the image of God, should shine on them. **5** For we do not preach ourselves, but Christ Jesus the Lord, and ourselves your bondservants for Jesus' sake. **6** For it is the God who commanded light to shine out of darkness, who has shone in our hearts to give the light of the knowledge of the glory of God in the face of Jesus Christ. **7** *But we have this treasure in earthen vessels,[2]* that the *excellence of the power[3]* may be of God and not of us. **8** We are hard-pressed on every side, yet not crushed; we are perplexed, but not in despair; **9** persecuted, but not forsaken; struck down, but not destroyed— **10** *always carrying about in the body the dying of the Lord Jesus,[2]* that the *life of Jesus[19]* also may be *manifested in our body.[3]* **2COR 4:3-10**

from the inside-out[3] in the blood-washed, New Testament believer. Just like the Israelites, *those who are still perishing[20]* (unbelievers) need to remain *veiled[20]* until they *believe[7]* and *receive salvation,[1]* because without being washed by the blood, the *unredeemed flesh[20]* cannot stand to have *the glory[3] of Christ[1] shine[10]* on it (2Cor 4:3-4).

The glory[3] of the law[24] was passing away because it could do nothing to sanctify the flesh, and by it, no man can be justified. It's called the *ministry of death because the letter of the law kills[24]*—its requirement is perfection or death (2Cor 3:6 p55). Its whole purpose is to *reveal the knowledge of sin[20a]* and highlight our need for our Savior (Rom 3:19-20, *The Finished Work of Christ;* Chapter 4).

> Now we know that whatever the law says, it says to those who are under the law, that every mouth may be stopped, and all the world may become guilty before God. Therefore by the deeds of the law no flesh will be justified in His sight, *for by the law[24] is the knowledge of sin.[20]* ROM 3:19-20

In juxtaposition, the *ministry of the Spirit and the ministry of righteousness[8]* is the *New Testament glory[3]* that exceeds much more than *the glory of the Old.[24]* The *dwelling place of the Spirit of the Lord[2] is where liberty is.[1]* For reason of the blood, the veil can be lifted. Not only can we stand in the presence of the glory of God, we are carriers of His presence and called to be *ministers of His power[3]* through the *ministry of the Spirit[2a]* (2Cor 3:8 p55). Yet even as the redeemed, our natural flesh can still be challenged to stand under the weight of the glory!

So contrary to the understanding that has been prevalent in the church, advancing *from glory to glory* (2Cor 3:18 p55) is not about experiencing a miraculous glory moment and progressing to a greater one. Rather, it's the privilege of having passed from the veiled *glory of the law[24]* to the unveiled *glory[3] of grace[5] by faith[7] in Christ and His Finished Work.[1]* Because we've been washed by the blood and we qualify to be filled with the Holy Spirit, we get to carry the very treasure of His glory in these earthen vessels (2Cor 4:7 p55).

This is the *glory[3]* of the *gospel of Christ![1]*

As Paul came to know very well, when we preach and unveil

For I determined not to know anything among you except Jesus Christ and Him crucified. I was with you in weakness, in fear, and in much trembling. And my speech and my preaching were not with persuasive words of human wisdom, but in *demonstration of the Spirit[2a] and of power,[3]* that your faith should not be in the *wisdom of men[10c]* but in the *power of God.[3]* **1COR 2:2-5**

But the *manifestation of the Spirit[3]* is given to each one for the profit of all: for to one is given the word of wisdom through the Spirit, to another the word of knowledge through the same Spirit, to another faith by the same Spirit, to another gifts of healings by the same Spirit, to another the working of miracles, to another prophecy, to another discerning of spirits, to another different kinds of tongues, to another the interpretation of tongues. But one and the same Spirit works all these things, distributing to each one individually as He wills. **1COR 12:7-11**

KEY GREEK WORDS

585 APODEIXIS:[2a] (ap-od'-ike-sis) A showing off, demonstration, proof

5321 PHANERÓSIS:[3] (fan-er'-o-sis) manifestation, disclosure, a "coming to light." See **5319 PHANEROŌ** to make visible, make clear, make known.

the mysteries of the gospel, God will witness to it with *glorious demonstrations of the Spirit[2a] and manifestations of power[3]* (1Cor 2:2-5):

The *demonstration of the Spirit[3]* results in *revelation understanding[10]* of His *righteousness by faith[8]* that dawns on, and transforms the hearer *from faith[24] to faith[8]*—from the unredeemed man attempting to *establish his own righteousness by the law,[24]* to New Covenant saint resting in God's gift of *righteousness by faith in Christ[8]* (Rom 1:16-17, Rom 10:3-4).

For I am not ashamed of the *gospel of Christ,[1]* for it is the power of God to salvation for everyone who believes, for the Jew first and also for the Greek. For in it the righteousness of God is revealed *from faith[24] to faith;[8]* as it is written, *"The just shall live by faith."* **ROM 1:16-17**

For they *being ignorant of God's righteousness,[8]* and *seeking to establish their own righteousness,[24]* have not submitted to the righteousness of God. For *Christ is the end of the law for righteousness[24]* to everyone who *believes.[7]* **ROM 10:3-4**

💧 The *manifestation of power*[3] is the result of the hearer speaking and acting in accordance to the faith that arose out of the *revelation.*[10] In other words, when we say *"Amen"*[7] to what was *revealed*[10] in the demonstration of the Holy Spirit, *true faith*[7] arises, *obedience*[2a] *is our automatic, divine response,*[7] and a *manifestation of His power*[3] is released.

Now as *the justified*[8] who perpetually live by *faith,*[7] we access His daily *provisions of grace*[5a] through this same demonstration of Holy Spirit *revelation*[10] and resulting *power*[3] (Rom 5:1-2).

THE SURE EXPECTATION OF THE GLORY

👣 The entire New Covenant is about *restoration to fullness of relationship with the Father*[2] and He's the one who is doing it in us (Gal 3:13-14 p50). By the blood of Christ, the love of God shed abroad in our hearts has utterly redeemed us from the curse. 💧 In fact, *the glory is the demonstration*[3] *of God's love poured out in our hearts*[1] *by the Holy Spirit*[2] (Rom 5:1-8), and this is why we can, and must have a *sure expectation*[31] of His *glory manifested in our life's challenges.*[3]

> **1** Therefore, having been justified by faith, we have peace with God through our Lord Jesus Christ, **2** through whom also we have access by faith into this grace in which we stand, and *rejoice in hope*[31] of the *glory of God.*[3] **3** And not only that, but we also *glory in tribulations,*[3] knowing that tribulation produces perseverance; **4** and perseverance, character; and character, *hope.*[31] **5** Now *hope*[31] does not disappoint, because *the love of God has been poured out in our hearts by the Holy Spirit*[1] who was given to us. **6** For when we were still without strength, in due time Christ died for the ungodly. **7** For scarcely for a righteous man will one die; yet perhaps for a good man someone would even dare to die. **8** But *God demonstrates*[3] *His own love toward us,*[1] in that while we were still sinners, Christ died for us. **ROM 5:1-8**
>
> ### KEY GREEK WORD
>
> **1680 ELPIS:**[31] (el-pece') Expectation, hope, trust, confidence. † *Expectation of what is sure (certain).*

† Helps Word-Studies

This promise of the Spirit is our **earnest deposit,**[2] our **heaven-backed guarantee**[2] of our **full redemption**[14] (Eph 1:13-14). His **glory**[3] is at work in us **continually restoring us from corrupted, carnal thinking**[17b] all the way to the **perfection of the New Creation,**[9] where we will be glorified at the **resurrection.**[14]

Reiterating this essential truth, the **glory**[3] in us **is** the manifestation of the love of God that has been perfected in us and **is transforming us into His image**[9] (2Cor 3:18 p55). Not that we loved Him which was **the impossible requirement under the law,**[24] but that **He first loved us,**[1] and proved it by the greatest display of love at Calvary (1Jhn 4:10, 4:17-19, Jd 1:20-21). We have this **sure expectation**[31] that His presence and **power (His glory)**[3] will continue to change us from the inside-out.

Even though we don't have everything Adam had yet, we still have it better. The glory on Adam was based on his obedience, so when **he disobeyed, he fell**[23] **and lost his covering of glory.**[3a] Now, the glory in us is based on **Jesus' perfect obedience**[1] and the

> Now may *the God of peace Himself¹ᵃ sanctify you³ᶜ* completely; and
> may your whole *spirit,¹⁶ soul,¹⁷ and body¹⁸* be preserved blameless at the
> coming of our Lord Jesus Christ. **1TH 5:23**

infallible love of God. We'll never lose it as long as our faith is in
Christ. *God Himself¹ᵃ* is bringing the fullness of our redemption to
pass, to *sanctify³ᶜ* us completely, *spirit,¹⁶ soul¹⁷ and body¹⁸* all because
of *His great love for us¹* (1Th 5:23).

Here is a summary of the *glory³* at work in us:

The glory *transformed¹* us
into the *New Creation⁹*
(Rom 5:1-8 p58).

The glory *empowers³* us to
walk¹² as a *New Creation⁹*
(Rom 6:4-5 p51).

The glory is the *large down-
payment or guarantee,²* and the
sure expectation³¹ of our *future
redemption at the resurrection¹⁴*
(Eph 1:13-14 p59, Rom 8:28-30).

> And we know that all things
> work together for good
> to those who love God, to
> those who are the called
> according to His purpose.
> For whom He foreknew,
> *He also predestined to
> be conformed to the image
> of His Son,¹⁴* that He might
> be the firstborn among many
> brethren. Moreover whom
> He predestined, these He
> also called; whom He called,
> these He also justified; and
> whom He justified, these *He
> also glorified.³* **ROM 8:28-30**

THE GLORY IN US FLOWS OUT FOR MINISTRY

If we want to be a participant in *the ministry¹³ of the gospel of the
glory of Christ,¹* (2Cor 4:4 p55, 1Cor 12:7-11 p57), we must come into
alignment with His calling and purpose. We'll learn how to minister
in the Holy Spirit *by yielding to Him,²ᵃ* not ourselves (*Total Saturation
in the Spirit-Empowered Life: Vol 3; God's Empowering Presence
Through Us*). He puts weight on what He's doing rather than what
we're thinking and planning. Everything that's part of the redemptive
plan of God and glorifies *Jesus' Finished Work,¹* we can confidently

place a *sure expectation*[31] on the *glory to manifest and empower*[3] our words and actions. Like a mighty rushing wind, the wind blows where it will; the water springs up from within, and flows out—this is *Christ in us,*[2] *the sure expectation*[31] *of His glory*[3] (Jhn 3:8, Col 1:26-27).

The *final resurrection*[14] of the flesh is when we will experience the completion of our redemption—spirit, soul and body (Rom 8:28-30, 1Cor 15:54). The *completing work of the Holy Spirit*[3a] is when we will be thoroughly *glorified,*[14] and forever dwelling in the fullness of His glorious presence.

> The wind blows where it wishes, and you hear the sound of it, but cannot tell where it comes from and where it goes. *So is everyone who is born of the Spirit."*[3] **JHN 3:8**
>
> the mystery which has been hidden from ages and from generations, but now has been revealed to His saints. To them God willed to make known what are the riches of the glory of this mystery among the Gentiles: *which is Christ in you,*[2] *the hope*[31] *of glory.*[3] **COL 1:26-27**
>
> So *when this corruptible has put on incorruption,*[14] and this mortal has put on immortality, then shall be brought to pass the saying that is written: "Death is swallowed up in victory." **1COR 15:54**

FIVE

THE OVERSHADOWING

Psalm 91:1 holds possibly the most essential key to walking in the Spirit-empowered life. For greater clarity, it would be better translated as "those who **continually dwell**[1f] in the secret place[1e] of the **Most High**[1a] will **consistently live**[2a] under the **supernatural empowerment of the Holy Spirit."**[3] So correctly understanding the **secret place**[1e]

> He who **dwells**[1f] in the secret place[1e] of the Most High shall **abide**[2a] under the **shadow of the Almighty.**[3] **PS 91:1**

and knowing how to **dwell there all the time**[1f] is the difference between supernatural life in Christ, and natural life which is subject to **corruption.**[20]

WHAT IS DWELLING IN THE SECRET PLACE?

We are **found in Him**[1e] when we receive eternal salvation and the gift of **righteousness by faith in Christ**[8] (Phl 3:9). Being in Him is also the **secret place.**[1e]

We can never lose our salvation or our **"in Him"**[1e] status, but we **consistently dwell**[1f] in the secret place by developing **healthy salvation thinking.**[1f]

> ... and be **found in Him,**[1e] not having **my own righteousness,**[18a] **which is from the law,**[24] but that which is through faith in Christ, the **righteousness which is from God by faith;**[8] **PHL 3:9**
>
> For if by the one man's offense death reigned through the one, much more those who receive **abundance of grace**[5] and of the **gift of righteousness**[8] will **reign in life**[19] through the One, Jesus Christ. **ROM 5:17**

🦶 This **doctrinally sound mindset**[1f] is continually focused on the understanding that it's **His gift of righteousness**[8] that qualifies us to receive every blessing, protection and provision by the power of the Holy Spirit. This is how **abundance of grace**[5] flows to us in our everyday life (Rom 5:17) and how we **continually dwell**[1f] in the **secret place.**[1e]

> Thus says the LORD: "Cursed is the man who trusts in man and *makes flesh his strength,*[18a] whose heart departs from the LORD. **JER 17:5**
>
> For we are the circumcision, who worship God in the Spirit, rejoice in Christ Jesus, and *have no confidence in the flesh,*[1d] **PHL 3:3**
>
> For though by this time you ought to be teachers, you need someone to teach you again the *first principles*[1e] of the oracles of God; and you have come to need milk and not solid food. For everyone who partakes only of milk is *unskilled in the word of righteousness,*[8a] for he is a babe. **HEB 5:12-13**

So, in order to *reign in life*[19] we must cease from works, not only to be *right in God's eyes,*[8] but from *self-empowered living*[18a] in every way, shape and form. We put *no confidence in the flesh.*[1d] Self-improvement is simply not in the vocabulary of the Spirit-empowered believer (Jer 17:5, Phl 3:3).

Causing us to be *ignorant*[10b] and unaware of this *first principle*[1e] of our faith is a subtlety of *deception*[21] the devil excels at. It's one of his *prioritized areas of attack*[21] because when we become skilled in the word of *righteousness*[8] we have a heightened awareness of its function in our day-to-day living (Heb 5:12-13), a massive threat to his dominion in the earth. Study *The Finished Work of Christ,* Chapters 2 & 3 for thorough understanding.

ABIDING IN THE HEARING PLACE

With a whole chapter devoted to this topic (*Total Saturation in the Spirit-Empowered Life: Vol 3; Chapter 2*), in short, *living under the teaching mantle of the Holy Spirit*[2a] is abiding in the *hearing place*[4] (1Jhn 2:27). This is the relationship God longs for us to eagerly submit to. As we seek moment-by-moment to be *taught by Him,*[2a] to spiritually perceive His wisdom, we are *using our free will to surrender to His will*[2a] and to *abide*[2a] *in Him*[1e] in the *hearing place.*[4]

> But the *anointing*[2a] which you have received from Him *abides in you,*[2a] and you do not need that anyone teach you; but as the same anointing teaches you concerning all things, and is true, and is not a lie, and *just as it has taught you, you will abide in Him.*[2a] **1JHN 2:27**

WHAT, OR WHO, IS THE SHADOW OF THE ALMIGHTY?

1 The first mention of the Holy Spirit is in Genesis 1:1-2. He was *hovering* [3a] over, or *overshadowing* [3a] the void. This word **7363 RACHAPH** conveys a reproductive covering like a hen that broods over her nest preparing to lay eggs. Then, at the *spoken word* [4a] of God the Father, He brought forth all of creation by His *power.* [3]

The Holy Spirit is the might of God, [3] the third member of the Godhead who is the *doer* [3] of the Word. He is the glory, and His expressions include the *resurrection power,* [3] the *anointing* [2a]

> in the beginning God created the heavens and the earth. The earth was without form, and void; and darkness was on the face of the deep. And the Spirit of God was *hovering* [3a] over the face of the waters. **GEN 1:1-2**
>
> **KEY HEBREW WORD**
>
> **7363 RACHAPH:** [3a] (raw-khaf') to hover. § Brooding (and fertilizing). ‡ Metaphor: bird hovering over its young. Suggests care, protection, and impartation of life.

and even the *virtue* [3] that flowed from the hem of Jesus' garment (look up Luke 8:41-56 to read the story). Essentially, the Holy Spirit is all of these names, descriptions and expressions. He is the *overshadowing* [3a] *creative force of God* [3] and He operates based on *His spoken Word.* [4a]

> Christ is become *of no effect* [18a] unto you, whosoever of you are justified by the law; ye are fallen from grace.. **GAL 5:4 KJV**
>
> Are you so foolish? Having begun in the Spirit, *are you now being made perfect by the flesh?* [18a] **GAL 3:3**

THE RIGHT TO BE BLESSED

Now having a clear understanding of how to *continually dwell* [1f] in the *secret place,* [1e] *and abide in the hearing place,* [4] Psalm 91:1 explains this is the way we *abide under* [2a] *the shadow of His might* [3a] being fully able to receive of His power. God *wants us* to have the security of knowing we have a right to every supernatural blessing provided by the Finished Work. It's the coming and going, entering by *faith,* [7] then *falling from grace through works and fleshly self effort,* [18a] that hinders our receiving ability. Back on cursed ground, we've *made Christ of no effect.* [18a] (Gal 5:4, 3:3).

§ Brown-Driver-Briggs, ‡ Berean Strong's Lexicon

◊ We don't lose our eternal salvation but we're not *abiding under the shadow of the Almighty*[3a] and the supernatural life will elude us.

HIDDEN BY HIS GLORY

In Colossians 3:3, being *hidden in Him*[3a] refers to our natural man and the corruption that still exists in the flesh *being swallowed up by the glory*.[3a] The shadow and type we can seek understanding by is that of the acacia wood of the Ark of the Covenant (Chapter 3). It was the (natural) material that carried

> For you died, and your life is *hidden*[3a] with Christ in God. **COL 3:3**

the presence of the Lord, yet it was *hidden*[3a] from view, being completely covered on the inside and on the outside with pure gold.

We are the *substance*[19] of this shadow and type. We are covered completely, inside and out, when we received both applications —the *completion of the Holy Spirit*.[3a] We're *hidden*[3a] *in Him*[1e] and God doesn't see our corrupted flesh, He just sees Christ.

PERPETUALLY ABIDING IN THE SECRET PLACE

> **16** that He would grant you, according to the riches of His glory, to be *strengthened*[3] **(KRATOS)** *with might* **(DUNAMIS)**[3] through His Spirit in the *inner man*,[16] **17** that Christ may dwell in your hearts through *faith;*[7] that you, being *rooted and grounded in love*,[1] **18** may be able to comprehend with all the saints what is the width and length and depth and height— **19** *to know the love of Christ*[1] which passes knowledge; *that you may be filled with all the fullness of God*.[3a] **EPH 3:16-19**

As we walk out our everyday lives *dwelling*[1f] *in the secret place,*[1e] *in Him,*[1e] we are *strengthened with might* (**DUNAMIS** *miracle-working power*)[3] in the *inner man*[16] (Eph 3:16-19). *Hidden in Christ,*[3a] we should expect to live the *Spirit-empowered life,*[3] being *filled with all the fullness of God!*[3a]

Even more than that, looking at the order and meaning of the original

Greek text, verse 16 of Ephesians 3 (p65) would be better translated "... that He would grant you, according to the riches of His glory, *miracle-working power* (DUNAMIS)[3] that would give you *dominion-exerting strength and power* (KRATOS)[3] from the *inner man.*"[16]

LESSON 2

REVELATION OF THE LOVE OF GOD

Ephesians 3:16-19 (p65) is just one example of the many times Paul wrote about how he constantly prayed for all his disciples to *comprehend*[10] (have revelation understanding of) the magnitude of *God's love poured out at Calvary.*[1]

When we just *begin* to know the *love of Christ,*[1] we are *filled with all the fullness of God.*[3a] We're not hindered by *faith-killing thoughts*[21] of self-doubt, since in Him, being *carriers of the power of God*[3a] has nothing to do with our performance and everything to do with His.[1] We'll access all the *fullness of God*[3a] by the faith that automatically arises from the *revelation*[10] of His love[1] (Rom 10:17). We'll live in the *sure expectation*[31] *of the glory,*[3] His power that arises in us and pours out in our circumstances (Col 1:26).

> the mystery which has been hidden from ages and from generations, but now has been revealed to His saints. To them God willed to make known what are the riches of the glory of this mystery among the Gentiles: which is *Christ in you,*[2] *the hope*[31] *of glory.*[3] COL 1:26
>
> **KEY GREEK WORD**
>
> **1680 ELPIS:**[31] (el-pece') expectation, hope, trust, confidence. † Properly, expectation of what is sure (certain).

> So then faith comes by *hearing,*[4] and hearing *by the* (RHÉMA) *word*[4] of *God.*[1] ROM 10:17
>
> **KEY GREEK WORD**
>
> **189 AKOÉ:**[4] (ak-o-ay') hearing. † Used of inner (spiritual) hearing, *discerning God's voice.*

🌢 The hidden mystery now revealed in us is described in Colossians 1:26 as *Christ in you,*[2] *the hope*[31] *of glory,*[3] and it is the *sure expectation*[31] to walk as *empowered*[3] *sons of God.*[15]

† Helps Word-Studies

With all of this clarity we clearly see Paul's heart and desire—if we have *revelation understanding*[10] *of the love of God*[1] we'll be able to perpetually *dwell*[1f] *in Him,*[1e] never looking to *ourselves,*[18a] and we'll *abide under the shadow of the Almighty,*[3a] fully expecting to be a vessel for the *miracle-working glory of God.*[3]

For more clarity, take a look at Ephesians 1:18-21 below with some of the different Greek words for *power*[3] highlighted.

> **18** the eyes of your understanding being enlightened; that you may know what is the *hope*[31] of His calling, what are the riches of the glory of His inheritance in the saints, **19** and what is the exceeding greatness of His *power*[3] (DUNAMIS) toward us who believe, according to the *working*[3] (ENERGEIA) of His *mighty*[3] (KRATOS) *power*[3] (ISCHUS) **20** which He *worked*[3] (ENERGEIA) in Christ when He raised Him from the dead and seated Him at His right hand in the heavenly places, **21** far above all principality and *power*[3] (EXOUSIA) and *might*[3] (DUNAMIS) and *dominion*[15] (EXOUSIA), and every name that is named, not only in this age but also in that which is to come. **EPH 1:18-21**
>
> ## KEY GREEK WORDS
>
> **1411 DUNAMIS:**[3] (doo'-nam-is) *Miraculous power,* might, strength. "Power through God's ability."
>
> **1849 EXOUSIA:**[15] (ex-oo-see'-ah) *Power to act, authority.* † Conferred power, *delegated empowerment.*
>
> **2904 KRATOS:**[3] (krat'-os) *Strength, might,* dominion, power; a mighty deed. † from a root meaning "to perfect, complete." Properly, *dominion, exerted power.*
>
> **2479 ISCHUS:**[3] (is-khoos') Strength, might, power, *force, ability.* † From the Greek root, **IS,** force and **2192 EXŌ** have—ha*ve the force to overcome immediate resistance.*
>
> **1753 ENERGEIA:**[3] (en-erg'-i-ah) Working, action, *in the NT, confined to superhuman activity.* † The root of the English term, energy. Power in action, *divine energy, used only of superhuman power.*

THE INTIMACY OF THE OVERSHADOWING

Mary was *overshadowed*[3a] by the power of the Holy Spirit in order to miraculously conceive so that Jesus was *born of God and of the*

† Helps Word-Studies

> **31** And behold, you will conceive in your womb and bring forth a Son, and shall call His name Jesus... **34** Then Mary said to the angel, "How can this be, since I do not *know a man?"[3a]* **35** And the angel answered and said to her, *"The Holy Spirit will come upon you,[3a]* and the *power of the Highest will overshadow you;[3a]* therefore, also, that Holy One who is to be born will be called the Son of God. **LK 1:31, 34-35**

Holy Spirit,[19] rather than of the *Adamic corrupted seed.[20]* The term she used in Luke 1:34, to *know a man[3a]* is used throughout Scripture as a term for sexual intimacy.

KEY GREEK WORD

1097 GINÓSKÓ:[3a] (ghin-oce'-ko)to come to know fully, recognize, perceive. Implies a deep, personal, and relational knowledge, such as the intimate relationship between a husband and wife, and the covenant relationship between God and His people. Sexual intimacy (Lk 1:34).

A husband and wife is the shadow and type, while our relationship as the *bride of Christ,[1e]* is the substance (Eph 5:22-32). The mutual *passionate pursuit[7d]* and *loving submission of our spiritual relationship[2a]* is even graphically described through the whole book of the Song of Solomon. The difference is our marriage with the Lord is of *one spirit,[2]* as opposed to one flesh (1Cor 6:17).

> But he who is joined to the Lord is *one spirit[2]* with Him. **1COR 6:17**

> Wives, submit to your own husbands, as to the Lord. For the husband is head of the wife, as also *Christ is head of the church; and He is the Savior of the body.[19]* Therefore, just as the church is subject to Christ, so let the wives be to their own husbands in everything. Husbands, love your wives, just as Christ also loved the church and gave Himself for her, that He might sanctify and cleanse her with the washing of water by the word, that He might present her to Himself a glorious church, not having spot or wrinkle or any such thing, but that she should be holy and without blemish. So husbands ought to love their own wives as their own bodies; he who loves his wife loves himself. For no one ever hated his own flesh, but nourishes and cherishes it, just as the Lord does the church. For we are members of His body, of His flesh and of His bones. "For this reason a man shall leave his father and mother and be joined to his wife, and the two shall become one flesh." *This is a great mystery, but I speak concerning Christ and the church.[19]* **EPH 5:22-32**

As we are *in Him*[1] and *He in us;*[2] His glory is the *empowerment*[3] He wants to deposit in us. To *be made perfect in one*[3a] (Jhn 17:20-23) may be better translated as "completed as one," or even *consummated*[3a] as one—yet another term of intimacy.

Paul acknowledged *being found in Him*[1e] by His righteousness, we have the privilege to *know Him*[3a] and *His power*[3] (Phl 3:9)—not just at the *resurrection,*[14] but understanding who we have been made to be *because of His resurrection.*[14] According to John 17:20-23, as we are *sent,*[13] the world will know it. How? They'll be witnesses of His *resurrection power*[3] in us!

> "I do not pray for these alone, but also for those who will believe in Me through their word; *that they all may be one, as You, Father, are in Me, and I in You; that they also may be one in Us,*[3a] that the world may believe that You sent Me. And the *glory*[3] which You gave Me I have given them, *that they may be one just as We are one: I in them, and You in Me;*[3a] that they may *be made perfect in one,*[3a] and that the world may know that You have *sent*[13] Me, and have *loved them as You have loved Me.*[1]* JHN 17:20-23
>
> **KEY GREEK WORD**
>
> **5048 TELEIOÓ:**[3a] (tel-i-o'-o) bring to an end, to complete, perfect, *consummate.*
>
> and *be found in Him,*[1e] not having my own righteousness, which is from the law, but that which is through faith in Christ, the righteousness which is from God by faith; *that I may know Him*[3a] and the *power*[3] *of His resurrection*[14] **PHL 3:9**

EMPOWERMENT FROM SUBMISSION

◊ Submission to His *overshadowing*[3a] is total *submission to His will.*[2a] This is the intimacy of the *Spirit-to-spirit relationship*[2] and the result is *a release of power in us.*[3]

In Luke 3:21-22, Jesus was essentially *submitting*[2a] to the will of God to carry out the *ministry of reconciliation.*[1] He *submitted*[2a] through the *water Baptism*[1h] and *then* the Holy Spirit

> When all the people were baptized, it came to pass that Jesus also was *baptized;*[1h] and while He prayed, the heaven was opened. And the Holy Spirit descended in bodily form like a dove *upon Him,*[3a] and a voice came from heaven which said, "You are My beloved Son; in You I am well pleased." **LK 3:21-22**

Now all things are of God, who has *reconciled us to Himself¹* through Jesus Christ, and has given us the *ministry of reconciliation, that is, that God was in Christ reconciling the world to Himself, not imputing their trespasses to them,¹* and has committed to us the *word of reconciliation.¹³* Now then, we are ambassadors for Christ, as though God were pleading through us: we implore you on Christ's behalf, *be reconciled to God.¹* For He made Him who knew no sin to be sin for us, *that we might become the righteousness of God in Him.⁸* **2COR 5:18-21**

So Jesus said to them again, *"Peace to you!¹ As the Father has sent Me, I also send you."¹⁵* And when He had said this, He breathed on them, and said to them, *"Receive the Holy Spirit.²* If you forgive the sins of any, they are forgiven them; if you retain the sins of any, they are retained." **JHN 20:21-23**

Behold, I send the Promise of My Father *upon you;³ᵃ* but tarry in the city of Jerusalem *until you are endued with power from on high."³ᵃ* **LK 24:49**

came upon ³ᵃ Him. From that moment He carried the *power to complete ³* the *work of His ministry¹³* that would reconcile the world to God (2Cor 5:18-21, *The Finished Work of Christ;* Chapter 10 Part 1, *The Ordination).*

On resurrection day, Jesus *sent the disciples in the same way the Father sent Him.¹⁵* As they *submitted²ᵃ* to the plan of God, they received the power to *minister¹³ the word of reconciliation.¹* When we *submit²ᵃ* to the plan of God to declare the Word we receive the same *equipping power.³* It's astonishing to realize we are even authorized to forgive (Jhn 20:21-23)!

In Acts 1 (Chapter 3) and Luke 24:49, Jesus commanded the apostles to remain in Jerusalem. They *submitted²ᵃ* to His word in obedience and the Holy Spirit *came upon them.³ᵃ*

We see the same language when the angel told Mary the Holy Spirit would *come upon her and overshadow her³ᵃ* and she would conceive (Luke 1:34 p68). The power in her was not *consummated³ᵃ* until she *submitted²ᵃ* to God's plan and said, *"Let it be to me according to your word."²ᵃ* (Lk 1:38)

Then Mary said, "Behold the maidservant of the Lord! *Let it be to me according to your word."²ᵃ* And the angel departed from her. **LK 1:38**

Sarah received power to conceive in her old age when she *believed*[7] God was faithful and she *submitted*[2a] to His word (Heb 11:11).

> *Through faith*[7] also Sarah herself *received strength (DUNAMIS) to conceive seed*, and was delivered of a child when she was past age, because she judged him faithful who had promised. **HEB 11:11**

Without the Baptism of the Holy Spirit, Peter was fickle in faith, word and deed. However, after the Holy Spirit *came upon*[3a] him at Pentecost, after he *submitted*[2a] to the resurrected Christ as He restored him, Peter had a strong *anointing*[2a] *of the glory.*[3] He *spoke boldly*[13] and *demonstrated the power of the Holy Spirit*[3] wherever he went. As people were *overshadowed*[3a] by Peter passing by, they

> **12** And through the hands of the apostles many signs and wonders were done among the people. ... **15** so that they brought the sick out into the streets and laid them on beds and couches, that at least *the shadow of Peter passing by might fall on some of them.*[3a] **16** Also a multitude gathered from the surrounding cities to Jerusalem, bringing sick people and those who were tormented by unclean spirits, and *they were all healed.*[3] **ACTS 5:12, 15-16**

were all healed. It wasn't Peter's shadow, rather the Holy Spirit which Peter had *submitted to.*[2a] Then, in turn, when people *submitted*[2a] under Peter's shadow, they were *empowered*[3] (Acts 5:12, 15-16).

🌢 In summary, *our spirit*[16] and *His Spirit*[3] are one in *perfect union*[2] because of the *Finished Work of Christ.*[1]

The overshadowing of the Holy Spirit speaks of *intimate personal relationship.*[3a] When we learn to *continually dwell*[1f] in the secret *place*[1e] of the Most High and *submit fully to His plan*[2a] we are *yielded vessels to the heart of God.*[2a] Our *passionate pursuit*[7d] and heart of *submission*[2a] to His heart will sound like *"Let it be to me according to your word."*[2a] Not only will we *know Him*[3a] more and more, but He will *know us,*[3a] and we'll have a *sure expectation*[31] of *consistently living*[2a] under the *overshadowing empowerment of the Holy Spirit."*[3a]

⬤ Now through depths of all this understanding, we can recognize all three persons of the Godhead mentioned in Psalm 91:1 (p62) —the ***secret place (being in Christ, or in Him),***[1e] the ***Most High (God the Father),***[1a] and the ***shadow of the Almighty (the power of the Holy Spirit).***[3a] One of the most potent scriptures in the whole Bible, and there we are, intimately right in the midst!

SIX
THE EXPECTATION OF TONGUES

What should we expect once we have been *baptized by the Holy Spirit?³ᵃ* What is our *prayer language³ᵇ* for and what does it do? Clearly understanding *the purpose of tongues⁴* in the life of the believer is essential for us to practice this powerful spiritual gift with focus, intention and *expectation!⁴*

THE GATEWAY TO ALL THE SPIRITUAL GIFTS

Tongues is the only gift we can turn on and off at will. Every other *spiritual gift³ᵉ* is distributed in a specific moment *as God wills* (1Cor 12:4-11, *Total Saturation in the Spirit-Empowered Life:* Vol 3; Chapter 4).

But we can, and should become yielded, *expectational⁴ vessels!²ᵃ*

🔹 It's important to discern that the gifts of *tongues and interpretation³ᵉ* in a public setting is different from our *personal prayer language.³ᵇ* Both public and personal tongues are the same operation. The difference is God uses one or more people to deliver a specific message to a congregation by these two *spiritual gifts³ᵉ together* because it's crucial the *interpretation⁴ᵃ* is given immediately so all can *understand.¹⁰*

There are *diversities of gifts,³ᵉ* but the same Spirit. There are *differences of ministries,¹³* but the same Lord. And there are *diversities of activities,³ᵉ* but it is the same God who works all in all. But the manifestation of the Spirit is given to each one for the profit of all: for to one is given the *word of wisdom³ᵉ* through the Spirit, to another the *word of knowledge³ᵉ* through the same Spirit, to another *faith³ᵉ* by the same Spirit, to another *gifts of healings³ᵉ* by the same Spirit, to another the *working of miracles,³ᵉ* to another *prophecy,⁴ᵃ* to another *discerning of spirits,³ᵉ* to another *different kinds of tongues,³ᵇ* to another the *interpretation of tongues.⁴ᵃ* But one and the same Spirit works all these things, distributing to each one individually *as He wills.²ᵃ* **1COR 12:4-11**

> **1 Pursue[7d] love,[13a]** and **desire spiritual gifts,[3e]** but especially that you may prophesy. **2** For he who speaks in a tongue does not speak to men but to God, for no one understands him; however, in the spirit he speaks mysteries. **3** But he who **prophesies[4a] speaks edification and exhortation and comfort to men.[13a] 4** He who **speaks in a tongue[3b] edifies himself,[13a]** but he who **prophesies[4a] edifies the church.[13e] 5** I wish you all spoke with tongues, but even more that you prophesied; for he who prophesies is greater than he who speaks with tongues, **unless indeed he interprets,[4a] that the church may receive edification.[13a] 6** But now, brethren, if I come to you speaking with tongues, **what shall I profit you unless I speak to you either by revelation,[10] by knowledge,[10] by prophesying,[4a] or by teaching?[13] 1COR 14:1-6**

EDIFYING THE BODY BY FOLLOWING AFTER LOVE

It's an excellent thing to earnestly desire to apprehend spiritual gifts. In 1 Corinthians 14:1, Paul was pointing out the way—*by pursuing love*[13a] (*Total Saturation in the Spirit-Empowered Life:* Vol 3; Chapters 3 & 4). Since the whole purpose of all *spiritual gifts*[3e] is for *edification of the body of Christ,*[13a] earnestly desiring to love the brethren is how God will gladly use us to operate in them at greater and greater depths (1Cor 14:1-6, 12-13).

Edification[13a] means to build up, like a house, and make (spiritually) stronger. Only when the body of Christ is firmly *edified*[13a] and established by both the LOGOS[1c] and RHÉMA *Word*[4] are we able to receive by faith all the benefits that Jesus won for us through His Finished Work.

This explains why Paul declares throughout 1 Corinthians 14 that *prophecy,*[4a] as well as *tongues with the interpretation,*[4a] is much more valuable *in a public setting* than

> Even so you, since you are zealous for spiritual gifts, *let it be for the edification of the church that you seek to excel.*[13a] Therefore let him who speaks in a tongue *pray that he may interpret.*[4a] **1COR 14:12-13**

KEY GREEK WORDS

1377 DIÓKÓ:[7d] (dee-o'-ko) to put to flight, pursue. † *Pursue with all haste, earnestly desiring to overtake and apprehend.*

3618 OIKODOMEÓ:[13a] (oy-kod-om-eh'-o) *to build a house,* of the building up of character, edify, encourage. † *Build someone up by helping them to stand/be strong.*

† Helps Word-Studies

tongues alone. He certainly wasn't saying we should never pray in tongues in church. To address this common

> Therefore, brethren, desire earnestly to prophesy, and **do not forbid to speak with tongues.**[3b] Let all things be done decently and in order. **1COR 14:39-40**

misunderstanding, it's clear by verses 39-40 that Paul commanded leaders **not to forbid praying in tongues.**[3b] Yet, for someone to stand up and address the church, **tongues must have the interpretation.**[4a]

> Otherwise, if you bless with the spirit, how will he who occupies the place of the **uninformed**[10b] say "Amen" at your giving of thanks, since he does not understand what you say? **1COR 14:16**

The whole discourse in Chapter 14 is about maintaining proper order and being sensitive to the **uninformed,**[10b] who are either unbelievers who have not received Christ, or believers who don't know about spiritual gifts and their operation in the church (1Cor 14:16). **Personal tongues**[3b] can be practiced sensitively in church, especially when all present are informed.

But let's look at the similarity between **prophecy**[4a] and **speaking in tongues**[3b] and see why prophecy is preferred in corporate meetings.

THE PURPOSE OF PROPHECY

Prophecy[4a] is the process of **perceiving a RHÉMA Word**[4] from the Holy Spirit for another person or congregation, and **interpreting it.**[4a] It's always based on **bringing light**[10] to the LOGOS,[1c] and it **edifies, exhorts and brings comfort to men.**[13a] **Tongues**[3b] and **interpretation**[4a] has the same result. A tongue is uttered, interpretation follows, and **the body is edified**[13a] through **understanding.**[17a]

So what about personal tongues?

WHAT EDIFIES?

Paul strongly emphasizes in verse 1Cor 14:6 that **speaking to the believer without revelation,**[10] **knowledge,**[10] **prophecy,**[4a] **or teaching**[13] *has no profit at all!* Conversely, **with the interpretation,**[4a] the hearer is **edified**[13a] **through understanding**[10] **the** RHÉMA **Word of God.**[4]

🜄 In the same way, Paul says in verse 4 (p74), **he who speaks in a tongue**[3b] **edifies himself.**[13a] How? The inference is clear—it's also the **interpretation of the tongue**[4] **that edifies us**[13a] as we pray in our personal prayer language. "He who prays in another tongue edifies himself" because we are supposed to **understand**[17a] **what the Spirit is saying to us**[4]**—it's the understanding**[17a] **that edifies.**[13a] Clarifying further, Paul instructs in verse 13 (p74) to pray that we would **interpret.**[3e] This applies whether we are seeking the public gifts of tongues and interpretation, or just praying in our personal prayer language.

Now using the same reasoning from verse 6 (p74), we can see that mindlessly praying in tongues **without seeking and purposefully listening for understanding**[17a] *has no profit at all!* Clearly, we must **expect to receive the interpretation,**[4] or **revelation**[10] of our personal prayer language. With it, we can **expect true Biblical faith to arise**[7] that automatically prompts **Spirit-inspired words and actions.**[2a] In fact the whole purpose of tongues, private or public, is to **understand**[17a] **what the Holy Spirit is saying,**[4] so we know exactly what to do and say in any situation.

> But you, beloved, **building yourselves up (**OIKODOMEÓ**)**[13a] on your most holy faith, praying in the Holy Spirit, **keep yourselves in the love of God,**[1] looking for the mercy of our Lord Jesus Christ unto eternal life. **JD 1:20-21**

Using the same word 3618 OIKODOMEÓ (p74), Jude 1:20 concurs **—as we pray in the Spirit**[3b] **we are edified,**[13a] our **faith grows**[7] and spiritual maturity from **Holy Spirit relationship**[2] is the result.

OUR PURPOSEFUL SUBMISSION TO RELATIONSHIP

Tongues is the primary tool we use to **submit to His teaching yoke**[2a] (Chapters 2 & 3). **Asking for, and expecting**[7d] **His wisdom,**[10] we're purposefully *submitting to His teaching mantle.*[2a] God gave us this gift with the ability to activate it of our own free will, but just like all spiritual gifts, the *understanding*[10] that we receive is *"as the Spirit wills"*[2a] 1Cor 12:4-11 p73). So as we exercise our will to *intentionally pursue*[7d] *understanding*[10] we're submitting under His leadership to draw out revelation, patiently waiting *as the Spirit wills*[2a] to show us. This is how we perpetually *keep ourselves in the love of God,*[1] always looking to perceive how His mercy through the Finished Work *provided everything we need*[5] (Jd 1:20-21).

> For with *stammering lips and another tongue*[3b] He will speak to this people, **ISA 28:11**
>
> My son, *give attention to my words; incline your ear to my sayings.*[4] Do not let them depart from your eyes; keep them in the midst of your heart; **PRO 4:20-21**

Once we understand the purpose of tongues, we should nurture our *heart's desire*[7d] to pursue powerful *personal intimacy.*[2a] It's our everyday *revelation*[10] *relationship*[2a]—*submitting,*[2a] *inclining our ear to hear,*[4] *and obeying.*[2a] By it, our spiritual ears and eyes become *more and more sensitive to His leading*[2a] (Isa 28:11, Pro 4:20-21).

THE SIMILARITY AND DIFFERENCE BETWEEN TONGUES AND PROPHECY

The outcome of both tongues and prophecy is the same—*hearing a word from the Lord*[4] (always in relation to the Word). Revelation and *faith that has a corresponding action*[7] is the result. The difference is, one is for public use and *edification of the body of Christ;*[13a] the other is for our own *personal edification.*[13a] Either way, *every word we perceive*[4] from the Holy Spirit and *speak out*[4a] is prophetic in nature.

We don't need to receive a word from a prophet to hear from God. That's Old Covenant. Back then, there was no *personal, Spirit-to-spirit relationship.*[2] God only spoke through the prophet, priest or king. Today, because of *Christ,*[1] *our direct connection is restored,*[2] and *tongues*[3b] finely tunes our *spiritual ear to perceive*[4] what He's saying.

INTERPRETATION OF TONGUES, NOT TRANSLATION

It's important to understand the difference between translation and interpretation. When we translate something, it's word-for-word. In contrast, interpretation is the act of conveying an understanding of what was said. So as we *expect to hear*[4] and *understand,*[17a] we shouldn't expect every word of our tongue to be translated.

Also, we don't necessarily understand in the exact moment we pray in tongues. This brings clarity as to why public tongues needs the interpretation right away. With our *personal prayer language,*[3b] the interpretation might come as our day unfolds, or an event comes to pass. Either way, we expect the Word to be quickened in our inner man and to have *spiritual understanding*[17a] about our life circumstances.

SEEING AND HEARING

⬥ With this insight, we can see why Paul prayed so often for the church to be filled with the knowledge of the Lord in all *wisdom and spiritual understanding*[17a] (Col 1:9-13). He knew all too well we needed our *eyes to be enlightened*[10] (Eph 1:17-19) and he knew that *praying in tongues*[3b] brings that *flash of light*[10] to our understanding!

For this reason we also, since the day we heard it, do not cease to pray for you, and to ask that you may be *filled with the knowledge*[10] of His will in all *wisdom and spiritual understanding;*[17a] that you may walk worthy of the Lord, fully pleasing Him, being *fruitful in every good work*[3d] and *increasing in the knowledge*[10] of God; *strengthened with all might,*[3] according to His glorious power, for all patience and longsuffering with joy; giving thanks to the Father who has qualified us to be *partakers of the inheritance of the saints*[1] in the light.[10] He has delivered us from the power of darkness[20] and conveyed us into *the kingdom*[26a] of the Son of His love[1] COL 1:9-13

That the God of our Lord Jesus Christ, the Father of glory, may give unto you *the spirit of wisdom and revelation in the knowledge of him: The eyes of your understanding being enlightened;*[10] that ye may know what is the hope of his calling, and what the riches of the glory of his inheritance in the saints, And what is the *exceeding greatness of his power to us-ward*[3] *who believe,*[7] according to the working of his mighty power, EPH 1:17-19 KJV

Interestingly, the Greek word for *enlighten*[10] is **5461 PHÓTIZÓ,**[10] which means to *illumine or give light.*[10] We instantly recognize the origin of the word, *photograph.*

Think of how a photo is created. A flash of light imprints onto light sensitive film and the result is a picture that we can see and understand with clarity.

> **KEY GREEK WORD**
>
> **5461 PHÓTIZÓ:**[10] (fo-tid'-zo) to shine, give light, illumine, bring to light, make evident, reveal.
> ‡ *Light symbolizes God's presence, guidance, and revelation.* Describes the transformative power of God's truth and *revelation of Jesus Christ as the Light of the World.*

As we pray in tongues, we become *light sensitive.*[10] Revelation of the **LOGOS** Word flashes onto our heart and we say, *"I see,"* as we receive *wisdom*[10] and *spiritual understanding.*[17a]

> But *without faith it is impossible to please Him,*[7] for he who comes to God must believe that He is, and that He is a rewarder of those who diligently seek Him. **HEB 11:6**

Our heart sees and understands. *Faith that pleases God*[7] (Heb 11:6) arises automatically, and causes us to be *fruitful in every good work*[3d] (Col 1:9-13). We grow in relationship with Him and access *His mighty power*[3] that's always working *towards us, in us and through us.*[3]

This whole process describes our *restored relationship.*[2] It's how we're *strengthened with all might*[3] according to His *glorious resurrection power,*[3] which is the Holy Spirit. We can walk through any trial with *patience,*[3d] even *burn long with joy*[3d] (Col 1:9-13) because we know we'll come out the other side *victoriously saved, protected and provided for.*[5a] This is how we're delivered from *darkness of understanding,*[20] and access the *inheritance of the saints*[1i] *in the light of revelation understanding*[10] (Eph 1:17-19).

Imagine for a moment, what would have happened if Paul didn't pray for the churches. Would they have received *wisdom*[10] and *spiritual understanding?*[17a] Would they have received *faith*[7] from *revelation*[10] and therefore, been *fruitful in every good work?*[3d] Would they all have

‡ Berean Strong's Lexicon

been strengthened by the might of God and have *partaken*[9] *of the inheritance of the saints*[1] *in the light*[10] *of spiritual understanding?*[17a] Keep in mind, this prayer was Paul's continual desire for the church wherever he went. If this was simply referring to our initial salvation all believers receive, why did Paul need to pray continuously? Clearly he was referring to us *walking*[12] *in our inheritance*[1i] *now.*[9]

🌢 Apply this significant question to us today; do all Christians experience total deliverance from the *power of darkness?*[20] We all *qualify*[1] to partake of our *inheritance*[1i] here and now by the blood of Christ, but *do we all partake*[9] (2Pet 1:2-4)? Clearly, the answer is no. Some get stuck in the *lust of the flesh,*[18] *natural corruption*[20] and *cares of the world*[17b] (Mk 4:19). It's not automatically appropriated by being saved. So to *walk*[12] *in our inheritance*[1i] this side of heaven, we must determine to seek and receive *wisdom*[10] by our spiritual eyes and ears that are *capable of spiritually seeing and hearing.*[10]

> Grace and peace be multiplied to you in the knowledge of God and of Jesus our Lord, as His divine power has given to us all things that pertain to life and godliness, *through the knowledge of Him*[10] who called us by glory and virtue, by which have been given to us exceedingly great and precious promises, that through these *you may be partakers of the divine nature,*[9] having escaped the *corruption that is in the world through lust.*[20] **2PET 1:2-4**
>
> and the *cares of this world,*[17b] the deceitfulness of riches, and the desires for other things entering in choke the word, and it becomes unfruitful. **MK 4:19**

PRAYING FROM UNDERSTANDING

An important point to note, in 1 Corinthians 14:13-17 when Paul said *"I will pray with the spirit,*[3b] *and also pray with the understanding,"*[10] he wasn't saying we should pray in tongues, then pray in our normal language. The instruction is to *pray from the understanding gained*[17a] by praying in the spirit. In other words, we pray *until we hear*[4] and *understand,*[17a] then pray out *what we hear*[4] using our *Scriptural knowledge.*[1c]

† Helps Word-Studies

13 Therefore let him who speaks in a tongue *pray that he may interpret.*[4] **14** For if I pray in a tongue, my spirit prays, but my understanding is unfruitful. **15** What is the conclusion then? *I will pray with the spirit,*[3b] *and I will also pray with the understanding.*[10] I will sing with the spirit, and I will also sing with the understanding. **16** Otherwise, if you bless with the spirit, *how will he who occupies the place of the uninformed*[10c] *say "Amen"*[7] at your giving of thanks, since he does not understand what you say? **17** For you indeed give thanks well, *but the other is not edified.*[13a] **1COR 14:13-17**

Just the opposite of suggesting we shouldn't pray in tongues in church at all, Paul reiterates the reason *tongues needs interpretation in public*[3e]—the body must be *edified*[13a] through understanding what the *Holy Spirit is saying.*[4]

REVELATION—THE PURPOSE OF TONGUES

> Rejoice always, *pray without ceasing,*[3b] in everything give thanks; for this is the will of God in Christ Jesus for you.
> **1TH 5:16-18**

Paul, who penned three quarters of the New Testament by revelation, points out his own prolific personal practice of *praying in tongues*[3b] (1Cor14:18). Certainly it's no coincidence. Like Paul, we should live *praying in tongues on purpose and without ceasing*[3b] (1Th 5:16-18).

18 *I thank my God I speak with tongues more than you all;*[3b] **19** yet in the church I would rather speak five words with my understanding, *that I may teach others*[13] also, than ten thousand words in a tongue. **20** Brethren, *do not be children in understanding;*[17b] however, in malice be babes, but in *understanding be mature.*[17a] **21** In the law it is written: *"With men of other tongues and other lips*[3b] *I will speak to this people;*[4] and yet, for all that, they will not hear Me," says the Lord. **22** Therefore *tongues are for a sign,*[10a] not to those who believe but to unbelievers; but prophesying is not for unbelievers but for those who believe. **23** Therefore if the whole church comes together in one place, and all speak with tongues, and there come in those who are *uninformed*[10b] or *unbelievers,*[20] will they not say that you are out of your mind? **24** *But if all prophesy, and an unbeliever or an uninformed person comes in, he is convinced by all, he is convicted by all. **25** And thus the secrets of his heart are revealed;* and so, falling down on his face, he will worship God and *report that God is truly among you.* **1COR 14:18-25**

Edified from receiving *revelation*[10] and *spiritual understanding*[17a] is how we are created to function in the New Covenant, *abiding in relationship*[2a] with the Lord.

THE IMPORTANCE OF TONGUES IN THE CHURCH

> **9** "Whom will he teach knowledge? And whom will he make to understand the message? Those just weaned from milk? Those just drawn from the breasts? **10** For precept must be upon precept, precept upon precept, line upon line, line upon line, here a little, there a little." **11** *For with stammering lips and another tongue*[3b] *He will speak to this people,* **12** to whom He said, *"This is the rest*[1d] *with which You may cause the weary to rest,"*[1d] and, "This is the refreshing"; *Yet they would not hear.*[4b] **13** But the word of the LORD was to them, "Precept upon precept, precept upon precept, line upon line, line upon line, here a little, there a little," that they might go and fall backward, and be *broken and snared and caught.*[4b] ISA 28:9-13

Going even further to prove the importance of tongues in the church, in 1Cor 14:21 (p81), Paul quotes Isaiah 28:11. While admonishing us *not to be immature in understanding,*[17b] he reiterates that it's through *tongues*[3b] that God speaks to us. The inference is clear—this is how we become mature in Christ, *hearing*[4] and *understanding.*[17a]

Isaiah foresaw exactly what's happening today (Isa 28:9-13). So many *refuse to hear*[4b] the Lord through seeking and practicing *tongues.*[3b] This passage is proof He provided it for us today, *the age of rest.*[1d] Those who *refuse*[4b] are *"they"* in verse 12, who are doing exactly as described —studying the Word, line upon line, *broken, snared and caught*[4b] in *natural knowledge*[10c] not seeking the *breath of the Spirit*[1g] through *stammering lips,*[3b] by which *Scripture*[1c] becomes *the living Word.*[4]

Back to 1 Corinthians 14 (p81), verse 23 spells out why we shouldn't loudly speak in tongues without interpretation when *unbelievers*[20] or the *uninformed*[10b] are present—it creates confusion. Yet verse 22 clarifies that tongues *is* for the *unbeliever*[20] for a sign. While prophecy is for the body of Christ, verse 24 expands—when the *understanding*[17a] of tongues is given, the unbeliever is *convinced and convicted.*[13a] Witnessing an unknown tongue with an accurate interpretation that reveals the secrets of their heart is proof the Living God is with us!

The power of tongues in the corporate setting, certainly is how church in the New Covenant is supposed to normally operate. Tongues and interpretation should be encouraged. Through it, all are *edified*[13a] in understanding what the Lord is saying to us right now.

LESSON 5

THE POWER OF PRAYING ACCORDING TO HIS WILL

We know the general will of God from Scripture. The big question is, how can we *understand God's specific will*[2a] in any given situation?

Receiving *understanding*[17a] from tongues, then praying from our scriptural knowledge *according to what we heard,*[4] is *praying according to His specific will.*[7b] We'll enjoy a life of great power learning to live in this continual posture. Not only do we *come into alignment with what the Spirit is doing,*[2a] but there's an *obligation of heaven to do what we ask when we pray according to His will*[7b] (1Jhn 5:14-15)! We can truly know we *have what we ask*[7b] (Mk 11:24).

> Now this is the confidence that we have in Him, *that if we ask anything according to His will, He hears us. And if we know that He hears us, whatever we ask, we know that we have the petitions that we have asked of Him.*[7b] **1JHN 5:14-15**
>
> Therefore I say to you, whatever things you ask when you pray, *believe that you receive them,*[7b] and you will have them. **MK 11:24**

THE TWO-EDGED SWORD

The focused process of *praying in tongues*[3b] over the LOGOS *Word,*[1c] expecting His RHÉMA[4] and then *speaking it forth,*[4a] is the *two-edged, or double-mouthed sword.*[4a] As we become skilled at using this important spiritual weapon, we become aware of how it *divides, separates and distinguishes*[3c] between all things that are of the *soul*[17] and *flesh,*[18] versus those things that are of the *spirit*[16] (Heb 4:12 p84, Eph 6:13, 17-18 p84, Chapter 8).

> For the ***word of God***[1c] ***is living***[1g] and powerful, and sharper than any ***two-edged sword,***[4a] piercing even to the ***division of soul***[17] and ***spirit,***[16] and of ***joints***[18] and ***marrow,***[1g] and is a ***discerner***[3c] of the ***thoughts***[17] and ***intents of the heart.***[16] **HEB 4:12**
>
> Therefore take up the ***whole armor of God,***[11] that you may be able to ***withstand***[7] in the evil day, and having done all, to stand... And take the helmet of salvation, and the sword of the Spirit, which is the **(RHÉMA)** ***word of God;***[4a] praying always with all prayer and supplication in the Spirit,... **EPH 6:13, 17-18**
>
> **KEY GREEK WORD**
>
> **1366 DISTOMOS:**[4a] (dis'-tom-os) ***double-mouthed,*** two-edged.

While ***thoughts***[17] come from the soul, ***intentions of the New Creation heart***[9] come out of our ***inner man***[16] that's in direct communion with the Holy Spirit. As we develop praying in tongues, discerning between the two becomes crystal clear. We develop a conscious awareness of what is ***spirit***[16] and what is ***flesh***[18] (*Total Saturation in the Spirit-Empowered Life:* Vol 2; Chapter 4). Our behavior and choices come into alignment with the spiritual things of God and His leadership. We are truly ***co-laborers***[2a] as we submit ourselves to His purpose (1Cor 3:9-15). Everything of the ***flesh***[18a] will be ***burned up***[3c] ***and won't stand in the end.***[25] But everything that is ***spirit***[16] gives ***life***[1g] and ***establishes the kingdom here by calling heaven to earth.***[26a]

> For we are God's ***fellow workers;***[2a] you are God's field, you are God's building. According to the grace of God which was given to me, as a wise master builder I have laid the foundation, and another builds on it. But let each one take heed how he builds on it. For ***no other foundation can anyone lay than that which is laid, which is Jesus Christ.***[1] Now if anyone builds on this foundation with gold, silver, precious stones, wood, hay, straw, each one's work will become clear; for ***the Day***[25] ***will declare it,*** because it will be revealed by fire; and ***the fire***[3c] ***will test each one's work,*** of what sort it is. ***If anyone's work which he has built on it endures,***[2a] he will receive a reward. ***If anyone's work is burned,***[18a] he will suffer loss; but he himself will be saved, yet so as through fire. **1COR 3:9-15**

BUILDING ON THE ROCK

Purposefully *practicing tongues,*[3b] continually edified by *revelation*[10] *understanding,*[17a] we're increasingly *built upon the foundation of Jesus' Finished Work*[1] (1Cor 3:9-15, Mat 16:17-18). Revelation upon revelation, the *gifts of wisdom from above*[10] are the bricks *that build us up*[13a] *on our most holy faith*[7] (Jd 1:20 p76). These *bricks*[10] construct *our mighty fortress*[1f] in Him. The rooms filled with riches are way beyond all natural comprehension, and we are *built securely*[13a] upon the rock.[10] (Jas 1:17, 3:17, Pro 24:3, Lk 6:47-48).

> Jesus answered and said to him, "Blessed are you, Simon Bar-Jonah, for flesh and blood has not *revealed*[10] this to you, but My Father who is in heaven. And I also say to you that you are Peter, and *on this rock I will build My church,*[10] and the gates of Hades shall not prevail against it. **MAT 16:17-18**

> Every good gift and every perfect gift is from above,[10] and comes down from **the Father of lights,**[1a] with whom there is no variation or shadow of turning. **JAS 1:17**

> But **the wisdom that is from above**[10] is first pure, then peaceable, gentle, willing to yield, full of mercy and good fruits, without partiality and without hypocrisy. **JAS 3:17**

> Through **wisdom**[10] **a house is built,**[13a] and by **understanding**[17a] **it is established;**[13a] by **knowledge**[10] **the rooms are filled**[13a] with all precious and pleasant riches. **PRO 24:3**

> Whoever comes to Me, and **hears My sayings and does them,**[2a] I will show you whom he is like: He is like a man **building a house,**[13a] who dug deep and **laid the foundation**[1f] **on the rock.**[10] **LK 6:47-48**

As *He leads us and guides us into all truth,*[2a] the Holy Spirit *illuminates the Word*[10] that applies to our specific needs. Becoming more and more sensitive to *hear*[4] and *understand*[10] His will, we have *His supernatural insight*[10] for every situation.

He *reveals*[10] things in heaven and on earth, seen and unseen. These are the *unique building blocks of the Word,*[1c] the stones that we need personally to be *built up.*[13a] This *continual revelation*[10] *of Jesus and His Finished Work*[1] as it applies to us is what holds all

He is the image of the invisible God, the firstborn of all creation: for **by Him all things were created,** both in the heavens and on earth, visible and invisible, whether thrones, or dominions, or rulers, or authorities—**all things have been created through Him and for Him.** He is before all things, and **in Him[1e] all things hold together.[1f] COL 1:15-17**

things together (Col 1:15-17). He progressively *shows us[10]* what *(natural) ear can't hear and eye can't see.[17b]* He knows exactly what *building block[10]* we're missing and what we need next.

SPEAKING MYSTERIES TO GOD

🔈 *Praying in tongues, we're speaking mysteries to God,[3b]* then the Holy Spirit *reveals them to us[10]* (1Cor 14:2). We can expect to *be shown great and mighty things[10]* that affect every area of our life (Jer 33:3). We'll *know[10] the things that have been freely given to us[5a]* by God (1Cor 2:12) because it's been given to us to *know the mysteries[10] of the kingdom[26a]* (Mk 4:11).

Mysteries are always mentioned in the context of God revealing them to us. He has delighted to conceal these hidden treasures so we could experience the joy of *uncovering them[10] in personal relationship[2a] with Him.[2a]* As we *ask[7d] for wisdom,[10]* we never doubt (Jas 1:5-8). He promised He'd give liberally. He's just waiting for us to *ask in faith and freely receive.[7b]*

For *he who speaks in a tongue does not speak to men but to God,[3b]* for no one understands him; however, in the spirit he *speaks mysteries.[3b] 1COR 14:2*

'Call to Me, and I will answer you, and *show you great and mighty things, which you do not know.'[10] JER 33:3*

And He said to them, "To you it has been given to *know the mystery[10] of the kingdom of God;[26a]* but to those who are outside, all things come in parables, **MK 4:11**

If any of you lacks wisdom, let him ask of God,[7d] who gives to all liberally and without reproach, and it will be given to him. But let him *ask[7d] in faith,[7]* with no doubting, for he who doubts is like a wave of the sea driven and tossed by the wind. For let not that man suppose that he will *receive[7b]* anything from the Lord; he is a double-minded man, unstable in all his ways. **JAS 1:5-8**

We are *the kings He has reserved this glory for,*[7b] and we who desire to search His depths will *uncover*[10] His treasures (Pro 25:2, Col 2:2-3).

◀ *The veil that caused spiritual blindness*[20] has been removed by the Finished Work. *God's treasures are unveiled,*[10]

It is the glory of God to conceal a matter, but *the glory of kings is to search out a matter.*[7b] **PRO 25:2**

that their hearts may be encouraged, being knit together in love, and *attaining to all riches of the full assurance of understanding,*[17a] *to the knowledge of the mystery of God,*[10] both of the Father and of Christ, *in whom are hidden all the treasures of wisdom and knowledge.*[10] **COL 2:2-3**

as the Holy Spirit continually reveals those things to come (Jhn 16:13). *Praying in tongues*[3b] *expecting revelation*[10] *understanding,*[17a] *in submission to the leading of the Spirit*[2a] is how we are designed to operate as *sons of God*[15] who have *the mind of Christ*[17a] (1Cor 2:6-16).

However, when He, the Spirit of truth, has come, *He will guide you into all truth;*[2a] for He will not speak on His own authority, but whatever He hears He will speak; and He will tell you things to come. **JHN 16:13**

6 However, we speak wisdom among those who are mature, yet not the wisdom of this age, nor of the rulers of this age, who are coming to nothing. **7** But we speak the wisdom of God in a mystery, the hidden wisdom which God ordained before the ages for our glory, **8** which none of the rulers of this age knew; for had they known, they would not have crucified the Lord of glory. **9** But as it is written: "Eye has not seen, nor ear heard, nor have entered into the heart of man the things which God has prepared for those who love Him." **10** *But God has revealed*[10] *them to us through His Spirit.*[2a] For the Spirit searches all things, yes, the deep things of God. **11** For what man knows the things of a man except the spirit of the man which is in him? Even so no one knows the things of God except the Spirit of God. **12** Now we have received, not the spirit of the world, but the Spirit who is from God, *that we might know*[10] *the things that have been freely given to us by God.*[5a] **13** These things we also speak, not in words which man's wisdom teaches but which the Holy Spirit teaches, comparing spiritual things with spiritual. **14** But the *natural man*[17b] does not receive the things of the Spirit of God, for they are foolishness to him; nor can he know them, because they are *spiritually discerned.*[17a] **15** But he who is spiritual judges all things, yet he himself is rightly judged by no one. **16** For "who has known the mind of the Lord that he may instruct Him?" But we have *the mind of Christ.*[17a] **1COR 2:6-16**

There is a common saying: In the Old Covenant, Christ is concealed; in the New, *Christ is revealed.*[10] This means that God concealed His mysteries in the *Old Testament shadows and types,*[19] all of which point to Christ. As we receive *wisdom and revelation*[10] of the *Finished Work,*[1] those *pictures*[19] *are breathed to life in us.*[19]

> Nevertheless when one turns to the Lord, the veil is taken away. Now the Lord is the Spirit; and where the Spirit of the Lord is, there is liberty. But we all, *with unveiled face,*[10] beholding as in a mirror the glory of the Lord, *are being transformed*[17a] *into the same image from glory to glory,* just as by the Spirit of the Lord. **2COR 3:16-18**

They are *illuminated in flashes of light*[10] on the tablets of our hearts until the *pictures*[19] are *fully formed.*[10] The *veil is lifted*[10] when we come in to Christ, but it's the *gradual renewing of the mind*[17a] that progressively *opens the eyes of our understanding*[10] (2Cor 3:16-18).

A great example of this is the two disciples who walked to Emmaeus on Resurrection day. (Lk 24:30-32). Meeting a "stranger" they had the *Old Testament pictures*[19] revealed to them by Christ Himself and the *revelations "burned within them."*[10] At the end of their journey as they took Communion together, the *veil was lifted from their eyes.*[10] Not only

> **30** Now it came to pass, as He sat at the table with them, that He took bread, blessed and broke it, and gave it to them. **31** Then *their eyes were opened and they knew Him;*[10] and He vanished from their sight. **32** And they said to one another, "Did not our heart burn within us while He talked with us on the road, and while *He opened*[10] *the Scriptures*[19] to us?" **LK 24:30-32**

did they realize the stranger was Jesus, but they understood the *Old Testament prophecies*[19] about Him and comprehended *salvation by faith in Christ*[1e] and the *power*[3] *of His resurrection.*[14]

SEVEN

THE PRACTICAL APPLICATION OF TONGUES

It's possible to pray, minister, speak and study the Bible, all in the *natural.*[17b] Only when we *incline our spiritual ear*[2a] and *speak what we hear from the Spirit*[4] is it truly spiritual. Through tongues and the *expectation to interpret*[4] we access the *riches of our inheritance.*[1i] The *intimacy of our relationship with the living God*[2] deepens and He saturates us with ever-increasing *wisdom.*[10]

Up to this point, we have firmly established the accurate doctrinal understanding of the *Baptism of the Holy Spirit,*[3a] and the purpose and expectation of *praying in tongues.*[3b] Now we are ready to receive the practical how-to's that are rarely taught.

First, if we haven't already, we must *receive* the Baptism of the Holy Spirit and the accompanying sign of tongues.

Second, we must learn how to push through the typical obstacles to practising our everyday conversation with the Lord.

BELIEVING AND RECEIVING OUR PRAYER LANGUAGE

Now we've meditated on, and received all we've discussed so far, there's nothing hindering us from *receiving the promise of the Father*[3a] (Luke 24:49). All we need do is *ask*[7b] (Lk 11:13).

> Behold, I send **the Promise of My Father upon you;**[3a] but tarry in the city of Jerusalem until you are endued with power from on high." **LK 24:49**
>
> If you then, being evil, know how to give good gifts to your children, **how much more will your heavenly Father give the Holy Spirit to those who ask Him!"**[7b] **LK 11:13**

Once we've asked the Father for the Holy Spirit in a simple prayer, Acts 19:6 is a basic format of how to receive:

1/ Paul *laid hands*[7] on them;

2/ The Holy Spirit *came upon them;*[3a]

3/ They *spoke with tongues.*[3b]

> And when Paul had *laid hands*[7] on them, the Holy Spirit *came upon them,*[3a] and they *spoke with tongues*[3b] and prophesied. **ACTS 19:6**

Here's how this might look in our situation:

1/ If we're in a group setting, the leader takes Paul's part and *lays hands*[7] on us. If we're in a virtual group, the laying on of hands can also be virtual, much the same as the Centurion who believed that Jesus needed to *only speak a word*[7e] and his servant would be healed (Mat 8:8). If we're alone, we can similarly just *receive by faith.*[7b]

> The centurion answered and said, "Lord, I am not worthy that You should come under my roof. But *only speak a word,*[7e] and my servant will be healed. **MAT 8:8**

2/ The part of the Holy Spirit will be done by Him, and He will *come upon us.*[3a]

3/ Our part is to *speak*[3b] *in faith.*[7] This is more simple than we tend to imagine, therefore it's important to explain a few misconceptions so we don't over-complicate it in our minds.

People often imagine that the Holy Spirit will take over their body and the unknown tongue will overpower them, but the Holy Spirit never controls us in this way. Tongues is the one gift we can turn on and off as we choose to enter into conversational relationship with the Lord. Notice in 1 Corinthians 14:15, Paul describes how he could stop and start and he willed. In same way as all other *Spiritual gifts,*[3e] it's the *interpretation*[4] we receive that is

> ... I will pray with the spirit, and I will also pray with the understanding. I will sing with the spirit, and I will also sing with the understanding. **1COR 14:15**

given *"as the Holy Spirit wills"* (Chapter 6, *Total Saturation in the Spirit-Empowered Life:* Vol 2; Chapter 4).

Now that we understanding this, our part described in step 3 is to step out in *faith⁷* by purposefully letting sound out of our mouth in *expectation.⁷* As we do, we'll find the Holy Spirit will fill the tongue and the language of the Spirit will come forth. To reiterate, *our part is to "speak"* by letting sound come out of our mouth. We can't sit in silence waiting for something to happen to us—that's not faith. We must *believe, receive and speak⁷ᵇ* (Mk 11:24).

> Therefore I say to you, whatever things you ask *when you pray, believe that you receive⁷ᵇ* them, and you will have them. **MK 11:24**

Now, don't overthink it. Just follow the Biblical instruction. You've asked God, and He said He would give the Holy Spirit to anyone who asks (Lk 11:13). For more help receiving your prayer language, reach out at *Faith@SpeakItPower.com.*

LESSON 7

PRACTISING TONGUES

The following is a practical guide on how to *incline our spiritual ear²ᵃ to hear⁴* when we pray in tongues:

1/ Maintaining Spiritual Focus

One of the most common obstacles to praying in tongues with intention, focus and *expectation⁴* is our tendency to *wander in our minds.¹⁷ᵇ* If you've ever started with a passion and a purpose, then twenty minutes later you realize you've been thinking about your list of to-dos for the last fifteen, you're not alone! We all have our Martha moments, sometimes a lot (Lk 10:41-42).

> And Jesus answered and said to her, "Martha, Martha, *you are worried and troubled about many things.¹⁷ᵇ* But one thing is needed, and Mary has chosen that good part, which will not be taken away from her." **LK 10:41-42**

👣 The gift of *tongues* [3b] is so potent on the lips of a hungry and spiritually-focused believer. The gateway to all the other gifts, we have this powerful weapon at the disposal of our free will. The devil hates it beyond measure. It's not surprising he does everything he can to *distract us and derail us* [21] from our true relationship with God. This also explains why tongues has been at the basis of so much controversy within the church from the very beginning.

So how do we *set our affection* [7d] *on things above* [17a] and not let our thoughts go all over the place? It takes practice, and like anything, we need to resist the frustrations that come with it and push through the challenges we will inevitably face (Col 3:1-3).

> If then you were raised with Christ, *seek* [7d] *those things which are above,* [17a] where Christ is, sitting at the right hand of God. *Set your mind (affection KJV) on things above,* [17a] not on things on the earth. For you died, and your life is hidden with Christ in God. **COL 3:1-3**
>
> He said to them, "Why are you afraid? You have so little faith!" Then He stood up. *He spoke sharp words to the wind and the waves.* [7e] Then the wind stopped blowing. **MAT 8:26**
>
> For the *weapons of our warfare* [11] are not carnal but mighty in God for pulling down strongholds, *casting down* [11] *arguments* [21] and every high thing that exalts itself against the knowledge of God, bringing every thought into captivity to the *obedience of Christ,* [1] **2COR 10:4-5**

Sometimes we need to *speak to the wind and the waves,* [7e] and root out thoughts that roll around in our *natural reasoning* [17b] and hinder our ability to focus (Mat 8:26). We silence *lying voices* [21] that say we can't hear our Shepherd's voice (*Total Saturation in the Spirit-Empowered Life:* Vol 2; Chapters 4 & 5). We recognize *distractions* [21] and *take every thought captive* [11] by comparing them to every benefit we have access to because of *Christ's perfect obedience,* [1] not ours. Keeping a patient mindset towards ourselves, we consistently *tear down* [11] every *argument of the enemy* [21] (2Cor 10:4-5). The Word in front of our eyes will prevail and our ability to focus will sharpen and increase.

2/ The Conversation

🌢 Contrary to much teaching, *tongues*[3b] should be practiced like any conversation—with a focus to *communicate and fellowship*[2a] with the Holy Spirit. Our conversation starter should be a *scripture*[1c] related to our current situation that we place in front of our eyes. Praying in tongues while muttering the Word, we *muse*[7a] upon it while we pose questions to the Lord (*Total Saturation in the Spirit-Empowered Life:* Vol 2; Chapter 3).

We can flow back and forth from *tongues*[3b] to our natural language. Wherever the *unction of the Spirit leads,*[2a] we follow the *rivers of living water*[4] (*Total Saturation in the Spirit-Empowered Life:* Vol 2; Chapter 1). Whenever we realize our mind has wandered, we gently bring it back to the LOGOS *Word*[1c] in front of our eyes.

When we recognize that *speaking mysteries to God*[3b] is a stream of conversation, not in words but in *understanding,*[10] we've caught the flow. Soon the tongue will fade away from consciousness.

3/ Three Levels of Progression in the Spiritual Flow

Let's look at the same components of a revelation in the flow of the *conversation of tongues.*[3a] First *knowledge,*[1c] then *wisdom,*[10] then *understanding*[17a] (*Total Saturation in the Spirit-Empowered Life:* Vol 2; Chapter 2).

TONGUES: We start praying (without ceasing).

THE WORD: From *knowledge of the* LOGOS,*[1c] we start with a scripture. *The Spirit prompts*[4] others that bubble up to our *conscious mind.*[17]

THE VOICE: The Holy Spirit starts to bring *wisdom*[10] as He highlights and draws our attention to specific areas, or words within the Scriptures. *He's leading and we follow.*[2a]

THE REVEALING: As we focus our attention on what He illuminates, more related scriptures come into view. This *dawning of clarity*[10] keeps expanding and progressing. Every time we go up a level, the new *conscious stream*[17a] takes over and the level below becomes less dominant. The tongues fade away from our consciousness, replaced by a stream of *pure revelation*[10] *and spiritual understanding*[17a] that keeps opening up to greater and greater levels.

> For our *conversation is in heaven;*[3b] from whence also we *look for the Saviour,*[7a] the Lord Jesus Christ: **PHL 3:20 KJV**
>
> "Come now, and *let us reason together,*"[3a] Says the Lord, ... **ISA 1:18**
>
> *looking unto Jesus,*[7a] the author and finisher of our faith, who for the joy that was set before Him endured the cross, despising the shame, and has sat down at the right hand of the throne of God. For *consider Him*[7a] who endured such hostility from sinners against Himself, lest you become *weary and discouraged in your souls.*[17b] **HEB 12:2-3**

◉ This process describes our *conversation that is actually in heaven*[3b] as we speak mysteries to God through tongues (Phl 3:20). We come and *reason with Him*[17a] (Isa 1:18) *setting our minds, our affections, on things above*[7d] (Col 3:1-3 p92). Always *looking unto Jesus,*[7a] the author and finisher of our faith, we *consider His perspective*[17a] and the salvation He provided us in all things. This is how we keep from slipping back into *natural thinking and becoming discouraged in our soul*[17b] (Heb 12:2-3).

◉ This is what our *conversation*[3b] looks like. While the *world*[27] and *carnal Christians*[17b] look to *their own ability,*[18a] trusting in the *world's resources that have an appearance of strength,*[27] *we look to the God of our*

> Woe to *those who go down to Egypt for help, and rely on horses, who trust in chariots because they are many, and in horsemen because they are very strong,*[27] but who do not look to the Holy One of Israel, nor seek the Lord! **ISA 31:1**
>
> "*Look to Me, and be saved,*[7a] all you ends of the earth! For I am God, and there is no other. **ISA 45:22**
>
> Therefore *I will look to the Lord; I will wait for the God of my salvation;*[7a] my God will hear me. **MIC 7:7**

salvation[7a] and in Him alone. We trust Him in every moment of our day-to-day existence (Isa 31:1, Isa 45:22, Mic 7:7).

STEPPING OVER INTO THE SPIRIT

John frequently spoke of being *carried away in the Spirit,*[3a] and *then he saw*[10] something way beyond the natural reality of the world (Rev 17:3, 21:10). Yet John was a man with a *Spirit-filled nature*[9] just like ours. If we *desire*[7d] *to know the Lord*[3a] with the same passion as the man who laid his head upon Jesus' chest, we can expect the same.

And he carried me away in the Spirit[3a] into a wilderness; *and I saw...*[10] (a woman sitting on a scarlet beast, full of blasphemous names, having seven heads and ten horns.) **REV 17:3**

And he carried me away in the Spirit[3a] to a great and high mountain, *and showed me...*[10] (the holy city, Jerusalem, coming down out of heaven from God,) **REV 21:10**

We need to *raise our spiritual eyesight*[7] to a much higher place. What *mysteries*[10] could we fathom and *walk in,*[12] here and now? There is simply no limit. We need to start by realizing we are not even scratching the surface!

EIGHT
THE BAPTISM BY FIRE

Hovering over the unformed earth waiting for the Word of God to go forth, the Holy Spirit's first action was to bring *chaos*[20] into *order*[1e] and *darkness*[20] into *light*[10] (Gen 1:1-3). ❶ Considering the law of first mention, we should view everything He does through this lens:

(1) He brings *divine order;*[1e]

(2) He brings *revelation light,*[10] or understanding;

(3) He reveals the *Word*[1c] which is about the *Finished Work;*[1]

(4) *Empowerment*[3] is the result.

> in the beginning God created the heavens and the earth. The earth was *without form,*[20] and *void;*[20] and darkness was on the face of the deep (abyss). And the Spirit of God was hovering over the face of the waters. Then God said, "Let there be light"; and there was light. **GEN 1:1-3**
>
> **KEY HEBREW WORDS**
>
> **8414 TOHU:** (to'-hoo) formlessness, confusion, chaos
>
> **922 BOHU:** (bo'-hoo) emptiness

This numbered list is referred to four times in this chapter, so keep your eyes open and make the connections. Now let's view the believer through this lens.

THE DIVINE ORDER OF THE HOLY SPIRIT

Before the *new birth,*[19] our being is *out of order.*[20] We function as body, soul, and spirit (in that order), where the *flesh*[18] is predominant and we're *ruled by its lusts and slaves to sin*[20] (Eph 2:1-3).

> And you He made alive, who were dead in trespasses and sins, in which you once walked according to the course of this world, according to the prince of the power of the air, the spirit who now works in the sons of disobedience, among whom also *we all once conducted ourselves*[12] *in the lusts of our flesh,*[18] fulfilling the desires of the flesh and of the mind, and *were by nature children of wrath,*[20] just as the others. **EPH 2:1-3**

Washed by the blood, the Holy Spirit enters and restores us to *divine order*[1e] —spirit, soul, and body (2Cor 5:17). Over time, our *spirit*[16] becomes dominant through our *willing submission,*[2a] and

> Therefore, if anyone is in Christ, he is a new creation; old things have passed away; behold, all things have become new. **2COR 5:17**

our *flesh*[18] is subdued. Through **(2)** *revelation understanding*[10] of **(3)** *the Finished Work,*[1] He brings **(1)** *order*[1e] to our thinking and His **(4)** *divine empowerment*[3] causes us to walk as New Creation saints.

All of this happens through the ongoing process of *sanctification by the Baptism by Fire.*[3c]

THE SANCTIFYING WORK OF THE BAPTISM BY FIRE

While the division of the wheat and the chaff in Luke 3:16-17 is widely understood as the separation of the child of God away from the sinner at the *end of the age,*[28] there is another important application of this picture to the believer now, in the *Church age.*[1d]

> John answered, saying to all, "I indeed baptize you with water; but One mightier than I is coming, whose sandal strap I am not worthy to loose. *He will baptize you with the Holy Spirit and fire.*[3c] His *winnowing fan*[3b] is in His hand, and *He will thoroughly clean out His threshing floor,*[19] and gather the wheat into His barn; but the chaff He will burn with unquenchable fire." **LK 3:16-17**

What the Fire Is, and What It Isn't

There are two operations at work when we receive the *completion of the Holy Spirit*[3a] (Chapter 3)—*the Baptism of the Holy Spirit,*[3a] *and the Baptism by Fire.*[3c]

Contrary to what many charismatic movements have suggested, the *fire of the Holy Spirit*[3c] is not a passionate, feel-good experience when we sense a supernatural wave of His power. Rather, it's the initial and ongoing work of the Holy Spirit that *separates and sanctifies*[3c] us, and brings us into greater and greater *maturity of our salvation.*[1f]

Contrary to other ideas about the fire, *sanctification*[3c] is not a process of improvement we undergo to be rid of sin in order to become better Christians. The separating process does involve dividing the *flesh*[18] from the *spirit,*[16] but it's crucial to clarify a fine line where there's much misunderstanding:

> Even though there is *another law working our members,*[20] (the corruption of the flesh trying to bring us back into captivity), sin has already been dealt with *by the blood of Christ*[1] (Rom 7:23-25).

But I see *another law in my members,*[20] warring against the law of my mind, and *bringing me into captivity to the law of sin*[20] which is in my members. O wretched man that I am! Who will deliver me from this body of death? I thank God—*through Jesus Christ our Lord!*[1] So then, with the mind I myself serve the law of God, but with the flesh the law of sin. **ROM 7:23-25**

> We're *not under the law*[5] anymore, so the *strength of sin*[24] has been removed (Rom 6:14, 1Cor 15:56-57).

For sin shall not have dominion over you, for *you are not under law but under grace.*[5] **ROM 6:14**

The sting of death is sin, and *the strength of sin is the law.*[24] But thanks be to God, who gives us the victory through our Lord Jesus Christ. **1COR 15:56-57**

> We're *not slaves to it,*[1e] *nor are we condemned*[1e] by it (Rom 6:6-7, 8:1-2).

knowing this, that our old man was crucified with Him, that the body of sin might be done away with, that we should *no longer be slaves of sin.*[1e] For he who has died has been *freed from sin.*[1e] **ROM 6:6-7**

There is therefore now no condemnation to those who are in Christ Jesus,[1e] who do not walk according to the flesh, but according to the Spirit. For the law of the Spirit of life in Christ Jesus has *made me free*[1e] from the *law of sin and death.*[24] **ROM 8:1-2**

If we do *sin,*[20a] *we have an Advocate with the Father—Jesus Christ,*[1b] the righteous, whose blood forever speaks of *our redemption*[8] (1Jhn 2:1, Heb 12:24 AMP).

> My little children, these things I write to you, so that you may not sin. And *if anyone sins,*[20a] we have an *Advocate*[1b] with the Father, Jesus Christ the righteous. **1JHN 2:1**
>
> and *to Jesus, the Mediator*[1b] *of a new covenant*[1d] *[uniting God and man],*[2] and to the *sprinkled blood, which speaks [of mercy],*[1] a better and nobler and more gracious message than the blood of Abel [which cried out for vengeance]. **HEB 12:24 AMP**

For more understanding of the *New Creation man,*[9] *sin*[20a] *and the purpose of the law*[24] in the New Covenant, be sure to thoroughly study *The Finished Work of Christ.*

So it's imperative to understand, life in Christ is not about sin anymore. As we submit to the process of *sanctification by the Baptism by Fire,*[3c] one of the effects is that we will walk less and less in fleshly, sinful behavior, but this is a *fruit*[3d] and not even the main purpose.

By the grace of God and *His gift of righteousness by faith in Christ*[8] (Rom 5:17), we are so much more than faulty humans doing our best not to sin anymore—not even close! In fact, the more we attempt to fix ourselves, we miss the whole point of the *substitutionary work of Christ*[1] and *fall from grace*[18a] (Gal 5:4). We become subject to condemnation (Rom 8:1-2), and come back under the power of sin and the flesh (1Cor 15:56-57, Chapter 5).

> For if by the one man's offense death reigned through the one, much more those who receive abundance of grace and of the *gift of righteousness*[8] will reign in life through the One, Jesus Christ **ROM 5:17**
>
> Christ is become *of no effect*[22] unto you, whosoever of you are justified by the law; ye are *fallen from grace.*[18a] **GAL 5:4 KJV**

Just the opposite, when we rest in the fact that it's the *Holy Spirit who causes us to walk in His statutes*[9] (Ez 36:26-27), our thinking is freed from the *law of sin and death*[24] (Rom 8:1-2 p98) and right behavior follows.

> I will give you a new heart and put a new spirit within you; I will take the heart of stone out of your flesh and give you a heart of flesh. I will put My Spirit within you and *cause you to walk in My statutes,*[9] and you will keep My judgments and do them. **EZ 36:26-27**

> To them God willed to make known what are the riches of the glory of this mystery among the Gentiles: which is *Christ in you,*[2] *the hope*[31] *of glory.*[3] **COL 1:27**

In truth, sanctification is the process that transforms us while the Holy Spirit unveils the *New Creation*[9] *to us,* which is *Christ in us*[2] (Col 1:27). As He reveals how completely we've been made free by Jesus' Finished Work at Calvary, we recognize *who He's already made us to be,* as opposed to something we're trying to become. By continual revelation of these truths, *He causes us to walk*[12] in the *power of the New Creation.*[9]

SUBMITTING OURSELVES TO THE FIRE

Whether we have received the Baptism of the Holy Spirit or not, the *Baptism by Fire*[3c] is the sanctifying work that happens in the heart of every believer. But it's through *praying in tongues,*[3b] received through the *Baptism of the Holy Spirit,*[3a] that we can *purposefully submit ourselves*[2a] to this transforming process.

It's the *God of peace, Himself,*[1a] *who is perfecting,*[3c] *renewing,*[17a] and *empowering us,*[3] bringing our spirit, soul, and body, into *order*[1e] and maturity (1Th 5:23). It's His *sanctifying Word of truth*[1c] that brings us *revelation*[10] of who we are because of the Finished Work (Jhn 17:17). Our part is to *fully submit*[2a] to this *process of sanctification.*[3c]

> Now *may the God of peace Himself*[1b] *sanctify you completely;*[3c] and may your whole spirit, soul, and body be preserved blameless at the coming of our Lord Jesus Christ. **1TH 5:23**

> *Sanctify them by Your truth.*[1c] Your word is truth. **JHN 17:17**

THE SOUND FROM HEAVEN

> **2** And suddenly there came a sound from heaven, *as of*[34] a rushing mighty wind, and it filled the whole house where they were sitting. **3** Then there *appeared*[4] to them *divided tongues,*[3c] *as of*[34] *fire,* and one *sat upon*[3a] each of them. **4** And they were all *filled*[3a] with the Holy Spirit and began to speak with *other tongues,*[3b] as the Spirit gave them utterance. **ACTS 2:2-4**
>
> "And it shall come to pass afterward that I will *pour out My Spirit on all flesh;*[3a] your sons and your daughters shall prophesy, your old men shall dream dreams, your young men shall see visions. **JOEL 2:28**

The day of Pentecost described in Acts 2:2-4 when the Holy Spirit was *poured out on all flesh*[3a] (Joel 2:28), is the subject of much confusion, division and controversy in the church. It's not surprising since it's impossible for the *natural mind*[17b] to comprehend this spiritual event. It's been literally depicted in paintings and taught in rudimentary terms, but anyone who has experienced the corporate anointing will agree the *presence and power of God*[3] is impossible to fully describe in words and pictures. So let's examine the scripture afresh through spiritual eyes:

> First, the *sound that came from heaven*[3] *sounded* like a mighty rushing wind. That doesn't mean it actually blew their hair and clothes around like they would on a windy day (Jhn 3:8). Yet, the *"wind,"*[3] or rather the *Spirit,*[3] filled the whole house and they were immersed in it.

TONGUES OF FIRE THAT SEPARATE

Then, it says, there *appeared*[4] to them *divided tongues*[3c] *as of*[34] *fire* which *sat upon*[3a] each one of them:

> **3708 HORAÓ** (p102) is the Greek word for *appeared.*[4]
> It suggests those present *perceived something spiritual,*[4]

101

> The wind blows where it wishes, and you hear the sound of it, but cannot tell where it comes from and where it goes. So is everyone who is born of the Spirit." **JHN 3:8**

as opposed to seeing actual fire. A way we could understand this is to consider how we can perceive the effects of wind but don't see the wind itself (Jhn 3:8).

What they *perceived*[4] was dividing tongues *like*[34] fire that *sat upon*[3a] them. Or, considering the definition of **2523 KATHIZÓ**, did it *make them sit down?*[3a] 🔒 The Old Testament shadow and type, or picture, of the outpouring of the Spirit at Pentecost was the glory that filled the temple where the priests *could not stand because of the power of God*[3a] (2Chr 5:14, Chapter 4).

No doubt, the disciples experienced the *heaviness of the tangible presence and power of God*[3] here in Acts 2 as well!

Not to be confused with *other tongues they spoke with*[3b] in verse 4, the *divided tongues*[3c] which sat upon each of them were described *as if,*[34] or *like unto*[34] a flame. In other words, their *perception*[4] of what was happening was *likened to*[34] flames of fire that continually flicker and separate—a description of an important *continual action*[3c] taking place.

KEY GREEK WORDS

3708 HORAÓ:[4] (hor-ah'-o) to see, perceive, experience, discern.
† *Perceive (inward spiritual perception).*

5616 HÓSEI:[34] (ho-si') as if, as it were, like

2523 KATHIZÓ:[3a] (kath-id'-zo) to make to sit down, to sit down, appoint, am seated, stay.

So that the priests *could not stand to minister by reason of the cloud:*[3] for the glory of the LORD had filled the house of God. **2CHR 5:14**

KEY HEBREW WORD

3519 KABOWD:[3] (kaw-bode') glorious. Weight, but only figuratively in a good sense, splendor or copiousness—glorious(ly), glory, honor(able).

By the definition and grammar of the word 1266 DIAMERIZÓ, we see that the *divided tongues*[3c] that sat upon them were actively *dividing tongues*.[3c] But what were they dividing?

KEY GREEK WORDS

1266 DIAMERIZÓ:[3c] (dee-am-er-id'-zo) to distribute, *to divide,* break up. Present, participle, middle or passive i.e. *Dividing tongues.*

In Luke 3:16-17, John the Baptist describes the *Baptism by Fire*[3c] using the shadow and type of the threshing floor.

DIVISION AND SEPARATION ON THE THRESHING FLOOR

John answered, saying to all, "I indeed baptize you with water; but One mightier than I is coming, whose sandal strap I am not worthy to loose. *He will baptize you with the Holy Spirit and fire.*[3c] His *winnowing fan*[3b] is in His hand, and *He will thoroughly clean out His threshing floor,*[19] and gather the wheat into His barn; but the chaff He will burn with unquenchable fire." **LK 3:16-17**

The *threshing sledge*[3b] was a farming instrument used to detach harvested grain from the stalk. The *winnowing fan*[3b] was a pitchfork used to toss the threshed crop into the air. The valuable grain being heavy, would fall to the ground and be gathered up, while the useless chaff being light, would be separated and blown away by the wind.

KEY GREEK WORDS

4227 PTUON:[3b] (ptoo'-on) a winnowing shovel or fan, a simple wooden pitchfork.

While this harvesting technique is the *shadow and type,*[19] the ongoing process of *separating*[3c] *our spirit*[16] to God and away from the *flesh*[18] is the *substance.*[19] Let's take a deeper look.

The wind represents the *Holy Spirit*[3] who does the *separating;*[3c] the grain represents *our spirit*[16] and all that is *of the Spirit;*[3] and the chaff represents *our flesh*[18] and all that is *corrupted.*[20] But what do the tools represent; the *threshing sledge*[3b] and the *winnowing fan?*[3b]

103

THE TOOL WE USE TO SUBMIT TO THE HOLY SPIRIT

Isaiah 41:15-16, a prophetic scripture about the second coming of Christ, contains an interesting reference to the threshing floor. It describes how He *makes us* *"into a new threshing sledge with sharp teeth,"*[3b] more accurately, a *two-edged mouth,*[3b] a reference to *praying in tongues.*[3b]

"Behold, I will *make you* into a *new threshing sledge with sharp teeth;*[3b] *You shall thresh the mountains*[4a] and beat them small, and make the hills like chaff. *You shall winnow them,*[2a] the *wind shall carry them away,*[3] and the whirlwind shall scatter them; you shall rejoice in the Lord, and glory in the Holy One of Israel. ISA 41:15-16

For assuredly, I say to you, whoever *says to this mountain,*[4a] 'Be removed and be cast into the sea,' and does not doubt in his heart, but *believes*[7] that those things he says will be done, he will have whatever he says. MK 11:23

KEY HEBREW WORD

6374 PIPHIYYOTH:[19] (pee-fee-yaw') tooth, two-edged. The same as 6310 PEH mouth.

Though there are other ways we can be separated and sanctified to God, Chapter 6 outlines how *praying in tongues*[3b] while meditating on (3) *the Word*[1c] is how *we* purposefully *submit ourselves*[2a] to the work of the Holy Spirit to bring us into (1) *His divine order.*[1e] (4) *Power*[3] to reduce *mountains*[4a] to dust is just one of the outcomes of our *faith*[7] that arises from (2) *revelation understanding*[10] acquired in this intimate and personal *relationship*[2] (Mk 11:23)!

Let's clarify this amazing picture in practical terms:

SHADOW: The *threshing sledge*[3b] and the *winnowing fork*[3b] prepare the crop to be *yielded and submitted to the wind*[2a] and the wind does the *separating work;*[3c]

SUBSTANCE: As we *pray in tongues,*[3b] we are *yielding and submitting ourselves to the Holy Spirit,*[2a] who *purifies and separates*[3c] our *spirit*[16] man from our *flesh.*[18]

SHADOW: The *grain*[16] and the *chaff*[18] are *divided by the wind.*[3c] The chaff is burned by *unquenchable fire*[3c] and the precious grain remains;

SUBSTANCE: Our whole man is continually *separated and sanctified*[3c] and purged of the residue of the sin nature. What remains is a greater and greater concentration of what is eternal—*the spirit.*[16]

A similar shadow and type that describes the sanctification process is the refining of gold or silver (1Pet 1:7, Pro 25:4). The dross represents the *leftover thinking patterns*[17b] from the *Old Man*[20] that hinder us from walking in the *New.*[9] As the fire *exposes, separates and removes*[3c] the *dross thinking,*[17b] the pure gold of the New Man is *revealed*[10] to us, in us and through us.

> that the genuineness of your faith, being much more precious than gold that perishes, though it is *tested by fire,*[3c] may be found to praise, honor, and glory at the revelation of Jesus Christ, **1PET 1:7**
>
> Take away the *dross*[17b] from silver, and it will go to the silversmith for jewelry. **PRO 25:4**

THE BURNING UP OF THE FLESH

Most of the time we are not even aware of the *purifying process*[3c] happening as the Holy Spirit *divides*[3c] between our *flesh*[18] and *spirit,*[16] but we clearly see the effects (like the effects of the wind, Jhn 3:8 p102). As the fire burns up the chaff, the power of the flesh is removed. Our tendency to *walk*[12] in the *self-empowered*[18a] *flesh*[18] loses its stronghold and the *fruit of the Spirit*[3d] automatically flourishes (*Total Saturation in the Spirit-Empowered Life:* Vol 2; Chapter 8).

Sometimes the fire is uncomfortable because it pokes at the flesh. It can bring conviction to our heart (but never *condemnation*[21]—Rom 8:1-2 p98) by exposing areas we've been unwilling *to submit*[2a] or are simply unaware of. The question to us is simple; do we want to continue to be controlled by the *strong urges of the flesh*[18] and answer its call, or do we want *God's purpose*[2a] and *power*[3] in our lives? *Having been set at liberty we are already free*[1] (Gal 5:1). Now, with our cooperation, He thoroughly purges us of everything that is worthless, if we allow Him.

Over time, we'll easily spot the *corruption of the flesh*[18] and *put it to death by simply yielding to Him*[2a] (Col 3:3-5). Instead of being led by the five senses and the lust of the flesh, what will remain is a *spiritual sensitivity to hear*[4] and *be led by the Holy Spirit*[2a] (Gal 5:16).

> *Stand fast therefore in the liberty by which Christ has made us free,*[1] and do not be entangled again with a yoke of bondage. **GAL 5:1**
>
> For you died, and *your life is hidden with Christ in God.*[1e] When Christ who is our life appears, then you also will appear with Him in glory. Therefore *put to death*[2a] *your members*[18] which are on the earth... **COL 3:3-5**
>
> I say then: *Walk*[12] in the *Spirit,*[2a] and you shall not fulfill the *lust of the flesh.*[18] **GAL 5:16**

REVELATION SANCTIFIES AND EMPOWERS

More precisely, *revelation*[10] from the Holy Spirit, that causes spiritual understanding, is the actual *dividing and purifying agent*[3c] in the process of the Baptism by Fire. The more *revelation*[10] we receive, the more *faith arises*[7] (Rom 10:17). The more we perceive that *we are already free*[1] by the Finished Work of Christ, we are *liberated from the behavior*[1] caused by the residue of sin in the flesh. The empowerment of the Spirit *requires our faith*[7]—when we come into agreement with the revelation of who we are in Christ, we are automatically empowered by the Spirit.

It's our *"Amen!"*[7] by which He causes us to walk in his statutes.

LESSON 10

TONGUES AND THE DOUBLE-MOUTHED SWORD

Entering into the *rest of the New Covenant*[1d] by faith in Jesus and His Finished Work at Calvary is how we're able to receive this incredible honor the Lord has bestowed on us—*the two-edged sword.*[4a]

Another millennial scripture, Psalm 149:4-6 is an eloquent description of the New Covenant saint. Beautified by *salvation,*[1e] joyful in the *power of His glory,*[3] singing praises from *having entered His rest,*[1d] we are able to receive and are *authorized*[15] to use the powerful *two-edged sword.*[4a]

The most well-known New Testament scripture about the *two-edged sword,*[4a] Hebrews 4:8-12 deepens our understanding about *entering into His rest*[1d] by faith in Christ, and echoes the dividing and separating work of the *Baptism by Fire.*[3c]

Typically, we've concluded the *two-edged sword*[4a] is the Word of God that we speak. However, *praying in tongues*[3b] over the **LOGOS** *Word*[1c] expecting to perceive a **RHÉMA** *Word*[4] of *revelation*[10] and *speaking it out*[4a] is a more complete understanding.

In other words, using our *prayer language*[3b] we submit to the Holy Spirit that *divides and separates*[3c] between *soul*[17b] and *spirit,*[16] between *joints (flesh)*[18] and *marrow (spirit),*[16] between the *(corrupt) thoughts of the soul,*[17b] and *(pure) intents*[16] *of the New Creation heart.*[9]

For the Lord takes pleasure in His people; He will **beautify the humble with salvation.**[1e] Let the saints be joyful in **glory;**[3] Let them sing aloud on their **beds (rest).**[1d] Let the high praises of God be in their mouth, and a **two-edged sword**[4a] in their hand, **PS 149:4-6**

For if Joshua had **given them rest,**[1d] then He would not afterward have spoken of another day. There remains therefore a rest for the people of God. **For he who has entered His rest has himself also ceased from his works as God did from His.**[1d] **Let us therefore be diligent to enter that rest,**[1d] lest anyone fall according to the same example of disobedience. For the word of God is living and powerful, and sharper than any **two-edged sword,**[4a] piercing even to the **division**[3c] **of soul**[17] **and spirit,**[16] and of **joints**[18] and **marrow,**[16] and is a discerner of the **thoughts**[17] and **intents of the heart.**[16] **HEB 4:8-12**

KEY GREEK WORDS

1366 DISTOMOS:[3b] (dis'-tom-os) **double-mouthed, two-edged.** † Like a "two-edged" sword with both sides of the blade sharpened to an edge; figuratively, what penetrates at every point of contact, coming in or going out.

4151 PNEUMA: (pnyoo'-mah) wind, spirit, breath.

◖ Then from *revelation*[10] we speak out the ***words** of the Spirit,* which is the ***Sword** of the Spirit*[4a] in action. It divides and separates *us* going in *(tongues)*[3b] and divides and separates *others* as it comes out (the RHÉMA *Word we speak,*[4a] or the *prophetic voice).*[4a]

Ephesians 6:17 even confirms that the *Sword **of** the Spirit*[4a] is the RHÉMA *Word of God which we speak forth,*[4a] and verse 18 confirms how we access it—*by praying always in the Spirit.*[3b]

1 Corinthians 14:12-15 not only proves that *praying in the spirit is praying in tongues,*[3b] but it also describes the intended outcome—to receive *understanding*[17a] from the Holy Spirit which is the same spiritual insight that *directs our praying*[4a] *with understanding.*[10]

Through *tongues,*[3b] we are *separated*[3c] to our calling. We speak out of our inner man and minister to others under the unction of the Spirit. The same *revelation*[10] that is part of the purifying work of the *Baptism by Fire*[3c] is what *edifies*[13a] and matures us individually and personally, corporately and ministerially.

> **13** Therefore take up the whole armor of God, that you may be able to withstand in the evil day, and having done all, to stand... **17** And take the helmet of salvation, and the ***sword of the Spirit,***[4a] which is the **(RHÉMA)** word of God; **18** *praying always with all prayer and supplication in the Spirit,*[3b]... EPH 6:13, 17-18
>
> **12** Even so you, since you are zealous for spiritual gifts, let it be for the *edification*[13a] of the church that you seek to excel. **13** Therefore let him who speaks in a tongue *pray that he may interpret.*[4] **14** For if I pray in a tongue, my spirit prays, but my understanding is unfruitful. **15** What is the conclusion then? *I will pray with the spirit,*[3b] and *I will also pray with the understanding.*[4a] *I will sing with the spirit,*[3b] and *I will also sing with the understanding.*[4a] 1COR 14:12-15

MAKING MELODY IN OUR HEARTS TO THE LORD

A greatly overlooked repetition of phrase from Psalm 149:4-6 (p107) echoes throughout the New Testament. The description of the New

Therefore do not be unwise, but understand what the will of the Lord is. And do not be drunk with wine, in which is dissipation; but **be filled with the Spirit,[3a] speaking to one another[13a] in psalms and hymns and spiritual songs,[4a] singing and making melody in your heart to the Lord,[3b]** giving thanks always for all things to God the Father in the name of our Lord Jesus Christ, **EPH 5:17-20**

Let the word of Christ dwell in you richly in all wisdom, **teaching and admonishing one another[13a] in psalms and hymns and spiritual songs,[4a] singing with grace in your hearts to the Lord.[3b] COL 3:16**

Covenant saints who have **the high praises of God in their mouth,[4a]** sounds very similar to **making of melody in our hearts to God[3b]** mentioned in Ephesians 5:17-20, Colossians 3:16 and other similar references like 1 Corinthians 14:15.

🌢 These phrases are always directly linked to passages **about tongues.[3b]** In fact, if we look closely, we can conclude the following:

Since when we pray in tongues we are **speaking mysteries to God[3b]** (1Cor 14:2-3), the prophetic psalms, hymns and spiritual songs that we **speak to each other[4a]** certainly come out of what we hear while

For **he who speaks in a tongue does not speak to men but to God,[3b]** for no one understands him; **however, in the spirit he speaks mysteries.[3b]** But he who prophesies speaks edification and exhortation and comfort to men. **1COR 14:2-3**

making melody in our hearts in relationship with God.[3b]

In other words, **tongues[3b]** and the **mysteries we speak to Him[3b] is making melody in our hearts to God.[3b]** Then from that praiseful melody, we **admonish and edify[13a]** each other with what we **hear.[4]**

With this understanding, it's amazing to realize how widely spoken of tongues is throughout the entire New Testament—way more than we have previously recognized. What a joyful description of how we

> Now in the church that was at Antioch there were certain prophets and teachers: Barnabas, Simeon who was called Niger, Lucius of Cyrene, Manaen who had been brought up with Herod the tetrarch, and Saul. As they *ministered to the Lord*[3b] and *fasted,*[3c] the Holy Spirit said, "Now *separate to Me*[3c] Barnabas and Saul *for the work to which I have called them."*[13] Then, having fasted and prayed, and laid hands on them, they sent them away. **ACTS 13:1-3**

enter into relationship with the Lord and surrender ourselves to His will.[2a]

In Acts 13:1-3, we see another indication. "As they *ministered to the Lord*[3b] and *fasted,"*[3c] they heard the *voice of the Holy Spirit*[4] and the important directive to *separate*[3c] Paul and Barnabas *for the work to which He called them.*[13] How did they *perceive His voice?*[4]

As we have already established, tongues is how He speaks to us (Isa 28:11, Chapter 6) and how we develop a greater capacity to *hear.*[4] It's not difficult to make the connection that *ministering to the Lord*[3b] is yet another phrase for *praying and praising in tongues,*[3b] and is how we can expect to receive important direction from the Holy Spirit.*[2a]

VESSELS OF THE TEMPLE

> For with *stammering lips and another tongue*[3b] He will speak to this people, **ISA 28:11**
>
> "For many are *called,*[13] but few are chosen." **MAT 22:14**

In this same passage, after fasting and yielding themselves to God, the Holy Spirit *separated*[3c] Saul and Barnabas to *the work to which they were called.*[13] In the same way, this work of the Holy Spirit that *separates*[3c] us away from the world and the flesh *sanctifies*[3c] us to God for a purpose—*His purpose.*[13]

It's one thing to be *called,*[13] but quite another to be *chosen, set apart*[3c] and *empowered*[3] (Mat 22:14). Just like the utensils in the temple were *separated*[3c] and *sanctified*[3c] for one purpose only—to serve God in the temple sacrifices—we too, are fully *separated*[3c] to God *to be used by Him*[13] (Chapter 4).

He **separates**[3c] us to His purpose by removing everything that hinders us from functioning in **His calling,**[13] primarily the **flesh,**[18] which is the greatest hindrance and distraction from spiritual relationship. As we **submit**[2a] through praying in tongues, He'll not just separate us **from the flesh,**[18] rather He'll separate us **to His purpose.**[13] In the **continual sanctifying work of the Baptism by Fire,**[3c] He's the one who empowers us to function in the spirit and He has given us this essential equipment to do the work of the ministry—**the gift of tongues.**[3b]

🜄 Through it, we become more submitted to our spirit than yielded to the flesh (Gal 2:20). The more we **pray in tongues**[3b] and meditate on **His Word,**[1c] the more **we know all things**[10] (1 Jhn 2:20). Our **thinking**[17] is unified to our spirit which is joined in **intimate oneness**[3a] with His Spirit (1Cor 6:17) and we become so connected to God, that our thoughts are His thoughts—**we truly have the mind of Christ**[17a] (1Cor 2:14-16). In this place of maturity in **intimate fellowship,**[3a] we are able to participate in **His purposes**[2a] and **manifest His glory**[3] wherever we go.

> I have been crucified with Christ; it is no longer I who live, **but Christ lives in me;**[3a] and the life which I now live in the flesh I live by faith in the Son of God, who loved me and gave Himself for me. **GAL 2:20**
>
> But you have an anointing from the Holy One, and **you know all things.**[10] **1JHN 2:20**
>
> But he who is joined to the Lord is **one spirit**[2] with Him. **1COR 6:17**
>
> But the natural man does not receive the things of the Spirit of God, for they are foolishness to him; nor can he know them, because they are spiritually discerned. But he who is spiritual judges all things, yet he himself is rightly judged by no one. For "who has known the mind of the Lord that he may instruct Him?" **But we have the mind of Christ.**[17a] **1COR 2:14-16**

COOPERATING WITH GOD AND GIFTS OF THE SPIRIT

In continual submission to purification and separation through the *Baptism by Fire,*[3c] we increase in our *spiritual perception,*[17a] and become finely tuned to *His leading.*[2a] Cooperating with the plans and

> for it is God *who works in you*[2a] both to will and to do for His good pleasure. **PHL 2:13**

purposes of God, we'll experience the greatest *manifestations of His glory*[3] in our own lives as well as the lives of others (Phl 2:13).

Purposefully learning to operate from this posture of *cooperation,*[2a] the church is full of the *glory of God*[3] and witnesses to Him in the most powerful ways, truly operating as vessels of God's presence in the earth.

Whenever we perceive a situation is out of order, we can know the Holy Spirit wants to bring it into *order.*[1e] We simply *cooperate with His leading.*[2a]

When we don't know how to pray, He brings *order*[1e] to our prayers and thinking.

When we lay hands on the sick, He brings flesh into *order.*[1e]

When we follow His leading, our steps are *ordered.*[1e]

All spiritual gifts function most significantly through the *separated,*[3c] *mature, yielded believer*[2a] for the purpose of helping others come into *order*[1e] so that they too can come into *submission*[2a] to Christ.

> *Pursue love,*[13a] *and desire spiritual gifts,*[3e] but especially that you may prophesy. For he who speaks in a tongue does not speak to men but to God, for no one understands him; however, in the spirit he speaks mysteries. But he who prophesies speaks edification and exhortation and comfort to men. **1COR 14:1-3**

To manifest *His glory,*[3] we just follow after love (1Cor 14:1-3, *Total Saturation in the Spirit-Empowered Life:* Vol 3; Chapters 3 & 4).

By *perceiving His direction,*[4] we'll know precisely what to do. Acting in *obedience,*[2a] *His power*[3] is released.

THE LORDSHIP OF THE SPIRIT

Whatever we submit to is what we make lord over our life. The more we give ourselves to *praying in tongues,*[3b] the more we are submitting to the Holy Spirit and *making Him Lord over our life*[2a] (2Cor 3:17-18).

> Now the *Lord is the Spirit;*[2a] and *where the Spirit of the Lord is, there is liberty.*[1e] But we all, with unveiled face, *beholding as in a mirror the glory of the Lord,*[1e] are being transformed into the same image from glory to glory, just as by the Spirit of the Lord. **2COR 3:17-18**
>
> *Stand fast therefore in the liberty by which Christ has made us free,*[1e] and do not be entangled again with a yoke of bondage. **GAL 5:1**

In this intimate relationship, beholding the glory of the Lord, *ever looking unto Him and His salvation*[1e] the more we'll comprehend and access the *liberty we're standing in*[1] (Gal 5:1).

Loosed from corruption, becoming ever more sensitive to His leading, the flesh becomes subdued, even silenced by the *ongoing sanctifying and separating of the Baptism by Fire.*[3c] There are no limits to how we will be used by Him for *His glory.*[3]

IMPORTANT NEXT STEPS

I truly believe *Total Saturation in the Spirit-Empowered Life* is one of the most important current day instructional teachings for the believer to rise up into the full measure of the new birth. This series practically guides us to live out of the Spirit and move away from our automatic soulish tendencies.

After the crucial foundations laid out in my book, *The Finished Work of Christ,* now our goal is to purposefully submit ourselves to live the way God the Father intended in the New Covenant. The entire reason He poured out His love by sending His Son to take *our* death sentence upon Himself was *so that* we could live in intimate, empowered relationship.

This series has 3 power-packed volumes:

> Vol 1; *God's Empowering Presence In Us* is a thorough commentary of the transforming work of the Holy Spirit in us, from the Old Man to the New Creation in Christ. We'll come to understand the life of God that thoroughly renovates our thinking, from non-spiritual to spiritual beings. With our cooperation, we cross over from living like sons of Adam, to authorized and empowered sons of God.

> Vol 2; *God's Empowering Presence With Us* unveils the evidence of the Spirit working in our everyday life. Engaging in a living relationship of Scripture and Spirit together, we'll come to expect Him to continually reveal the Word and quicken our thinking. We'll learn that as a New Creation saint, we're meant to have a constant, conscious awareness of being one spirit with the God of all Creation.

Vol 3; *God's Empowering Presence* <u>*Through Us*</u> dives deep into the gifts of the Spirit and all aspects of how He works through us to reach the world around us. This is not just for a few called to ministry. Every believer must be equipped for the work of the ministry to be God's ambassadors who bring His empowering presence everywhere we go (Eph 4:12).

I know you will be thoroughly transformed by this series. To reap every benefit as New Creation believers and joint heirs with Christ, I highly recommend submersing yourself in the group studies for each volume. You can do them by yourself, or by finding and joining a group Online. Even better, get these essential truths deep in your spirit by starting a group in your church or home. I'll personally train you to be an effective group leader and even lead some of your meetings. Visit *SpeakItPower.com/groups*

For more resources, including *Speak It:® 30 Days of Saturation in Healing* and *The Finished Work of Christ*, visit *SpeakItPower.com.*

Blessings!

LIVING WORD CONCEPTS

1 The Finished Work of Christ: the great exchange; the substitutionary work of Christ; the blood of Christ poured out at Calvary; the Cross; the gift of God, not of works; the chastisement for our peace was upon Him; He was wounded for our transgressions; by His stripes, we were healed; His great love with which He loved us; the love of God poured out at Calvary; the love of God shed abroad in our hearts; God demonstrates His love toward us in that while we were still sinners Christ died for us; the truth that sets us free; our victory in Christ; His victory that has overcome the world (**27**); the ministry of reconciliation; He who did not spare His own Son; for God so loved the world; grace-filled truth about Jesus; the gospel of grace; He yearns for us; His desire to woo us into relationship (**2**); God reconciling us to Himself (relates to the word of reconciliation that we preach **13**); peace with God through Christ; the gospel of peace; the fulfillment of the law (**24**); having become a curse for us, He redeemed us from the curse of the law (related to **20** and **24**); the obedience of Christ (vs Adam's disobedience **23**); one man's obedience; the truth the Holy Spirit leads us and guides us in (**2a**); Jesus crushed the head of the serpent

1a God the Father: the Most High; Jehovah Jireh; Jehovah Rapha; Almighty God; the living God; the God of all creation; Abba Father; God is love; for He is love; love is the substance of who He is; the Father of lights (**10**), the God of peace, Himself; the propagator of lights; the originator of lights

1b Jesus: the Messiah (who carried out **1**); our Lord and Savior; the Word made flesh (**1c**); lamb of God; He who takes away the sin of the world; our spotless lamb; He Himself is our peace; the Christ; the Anointed One; **5547 Christos** from **5548 xríō** (oil **3a**); the Way the truth and the life; the Good Shepherd; the door; the Bread of Life; the children's bread; the Lord of glory; the cornerstone; stone for a foundation, a tried stone, a sure foundation; no other foundation; our Advocate with the Father; our intercessor; the Lord of hosts; every knee will bow and every tongue confess that Jesus Christ is Lord

1c The written Word of God: the Bible; the established principles of the kingdom of God; the logos; Scripture; the Word that is forever settled in heaven; the Word of truth; the Word of God; the sanctifying (**3c**) Word of truth; **5198 hugiainó** healthy doctrine; sound doctrine produces **1f**; knowledge of the Word (**1c**) + the breath of the Holy Spirit (**4**) = revelation (**10**) understanding (**17a**); Biblical knowledge; Scriptural interpretation; the seed of the Word sown; the belt of truth (part of **11**)

1d The rest of God: entering into His rest; the New Covenant (made possible because of **1**); New Covenant reality; entering into the promised land; God sat down on the 7th day; Jesus sat down at the right hand of the Father; it is finished; we cease from works to enter into His rest; cease from self-empowered living (**18a**); repentance from dead works (**18a**) and (instead) of faith (**7**) towards God; the age of rest; the acceptable year of the Lord; Jubilee; the age of grace; the Church age; relates to the yoke of **2a**; the New Covenant that has made the law obsolete; we put no confidence in the flesh (opposite of **18a**); cast all our cares upon Him; the Lord will be your confidence

1e Salvation: Washed by the blood of Christ by faith in Christ; the transforming work of salvation by the blood; saved from wrath (**20**); made perfect by the love of God; those who are saved; the Saints; the Bride of Christ; salvation **4991 soteria;** save **4982 sozo;** being found in Him (not having our own righteousness **18a** which is by the law **24**); the secret place; in Christ; in right-standing (**8**) with God the Father; the first principles of the oracles of God; elementary principles of Christ; the foundation of repentance from dead works and of faith toward God; the upright; the blameless; divine order; members of the household of God; no longer slaves of sin; no condemnation in Christ; liberty in Christ; the liberty by which Christ has made us free; against such there is no law; there's no law speaking against us; he who has died has been freed from sin; free from the law of sin and death (**24**); wells of salvation

1f Salvation thinking: saved thinking; **4993 sóphroneó;** sound mind; **5198 hugiainó** healthy thinking from healthy doctrine (**1c**) causes us to successfully stand in faith (**7**); same as helmet of salvation (**11**); relates to **13a** because salvation thinking results in being edified/built up; New Covenant thinking; there is no fear in love; but perfect love casts out fear, sober; free from illusion and intoxicating influences; **3525 néphó;** sober Biblical judgment; those who consistently dwell in the secret place (**1e**); (opposite of **17b** natural thinking and the cares of the world that choke the Word; Crown of Thorns; our mighty fortress in Him (**1e**); thinking rightly about our salvation (**1e**); the spirit of wisdom and revelation (**10**) in the knowledge of Christ; rightly dividing sound Biblical truth (**3718 orthotomeó);** test the spirits, whether they are of God; in the world but not of it; we learn to abase and to abound; determine to only know Christ and Him crucified

1g Life: the breath of God; **2222 zoé;** the breath of life to create salvation (**1e**); everlasting life; eternal life; He breathed into Adam to become a living soul; Jesus breathed in them; **1720 emphusaó;** the new birth; born again (relates to **1**, **2** and **16**); born of the Spirit; alive to God; in Him was life, and the life was the light (**10**) of men; Jesus is the life that gives us light (**10**); He came to give us life, and life more abundantly; the life is our fellowship restored (**2**) with God; opposite is death and separation (**20**) from God; vitality; of the absolute fullness of life; life preserved in the midst of perils with a suggestion of vigor; Hebrew letter hey (number **5**—grace); Abram to Abraham; Sarai to Sarah; reign in life; relates to **3** because it has a suggestion of God's empowerment; more light (**10**) = more life; tree of life; you hath he quickened; made alive in Christ; resurrection from death; marrow (the source of life is in the blood/marrow); all Scripture (**1c**) is God-breathed

1h Water Baptism: John's Baptism; baptized in the name of the Lord Jesus

1i The riches of the glory of His inheritance in the saints; He has made us kings and priests; they which receive abundance of grace and of the gift of righteousness shall reign in life by One, Jesus Christ; our possession in Christ; joint heirs with Christ (relates to our authority **15**)

2 Restored Spirit-to-spirit relationship: His abiding presence; the automatic infilling after the new birth (**1g**); if we love one another, God abides in us; the Spirit in us; Christ in you (the hope of glory **3**); sealed with the Holy Spirit; the down-payment (guarantee) of our inheritance (**1i**); now we have received the Spirit who is from God; our body is the temple of the Living God; I in them and You in Me; be one in Christ and the Father by the Holy Spirit, joined to the Lord and one spirit with the Lord; made perfect in one; no longer I that lives but Christ who lives in me; He'll never leave us or forsake us; infilling of the Spirit; restoration of fellowship; face-to-face relationship; towards **4314 pros;** intimate communion (**3a**); our personal knowledge of God (and His Finished Work); the law of the Spirit of life in Christ Jesus; born of the Spirit; in the Spirit; (relates to **26a** the kingdom of God within us;) the dwelling place of the Spirit of the Lord

2a Submitting to the leadership of the Spirit: the yoke of the New Covenant; the yoke that is easy and light; yoked together with the Holy Spirit; the learning yoke; learn from Me; living according to the Spirit; we do not need that anyone teach us; He leads us and guides us into all truth; the Spirit of truth; yielded vessels to the heart of God; the love of God (**1a**) is now the life force (**1g**) behind all we are; Paraclete **3875 paraklétos;** called alongside; Helper; Counselor; Comforter; Advocate; teacher; the Lord is my Helper; the Spirit helps us in our weaknesses; another of the same kind **243 allos** (as opposed to **2087 heteros,** another of a different kind); those who are led by the Spirit (are sons of God **15**); revelation relationship (directly related to **10**); the teaching ministry of the Holy Spirit (by which we know all things **10**); just as it has taught us, we abide in Him; (saturated by the oil **3a** of God) we are receptive and anointed to understand His will; anointed (with oil **3a**); the anointing **5545 chrisma;** demonstrations (**585 apodeixis**) of the Spirit (and power **3**); submission to God's will; submission to God's purpose; willing submission to His leadership; submission to the Holy Spirit; sow (**26b**) to the Spirit; surrender; willing obedience; bondservant; obedience in the New Covenant is submission to His leadership; relates to **4** because we hear and only do what we hear Him say; hearing (**4**) causes our spiritual relationship to become mature; those of full-age because their spiritual senses (**16**) are exercised to hear (**4**); passionate surrender; co-laborers; the abiding place; abiding in the vine; He abides with us; walking according to the Spirit; good works (that produce fruit **3d**) that come out of submitting to His leadership (vs dead works **18a** that come out of self-effort); good works that endure the fire (**25**);

we are His workmanship created in Christ Jesus for good works; it's God Himself who is establishing us in every good Word and work; we are an epistle of Christ written by the Spirit; it is God who works in you both to will and to do for His good pleasure

3 The Glory of God: the Holy Spirit; **7307 ruach;** the resurrection power; **3519 kabowd; 1391 doxa;** the creative power of God; the tangible, visible presence and power of God; the sound that came from heaven like a rushing mighty wind; the Spirit-empowered life; the power of His right hand; (Christ in you **2**) the hope (sure expectation **31**) of glory; the same Spirit that rose Christ from the dead; Christ was raised from the dead by the glory; supernatural power; the shadow of the Almighty; the glory cloud in the desert; the pillar of fire at night; a consuming fire; the unspoken manifestation of God; the glory filled the temple; Moses face shone with the glory; manifestations (**5321 phanerósis**) of power **1411 dunamis**; the works that He did we will do also; greater works; strengthened by the might of God **2904 kratos,** the strength of God **2479 ischus;** the virtue that flowed from the hem of the garment; strong in the Lord and the power of His might; divine working **1753 energeia;** signs and wonders; healing; divine health; miracles; God working in us to produce an outworking of our salvation (**1**); power of salvation; outward action; from the inner man (**16**) to the outer man; being transformed into His image; appropriated; bring it to pass; manifestations of our inheritance; that you may be able (to stand **7**); ability; normal supernatural life in Christ; (demonstrations of the Spirit **2a**) and power; His mighty power that is always working toward us, in us and through us

3a Baptism of the Holy Spirit: the Spirit upon us; His Spirit immersing us/enveloping us from the outside; He commanded them not to depart from Jerusalem but to wait for the Promise of the Father; the Spirit poured out on all flesh; the Spirit of the Lord is upon Me; endued with power upon **1746 enduo;** clothed in the glory; crowned with glory and honor; encircled **5849 atar;** the Spirit poured out on all flesh; walk (**12**) in the Spirit (**3**); walking (**12**) in the wind (**3**); the evening breeze; the overshadowing **7363 rachaph;** to know **1097 ginóskó** (intimacy **2**); be filled **4137 pléroó**, mostly translated as filled (filled to capacity, completed to the maximum extent **4130 pléthó**), but better translated as completed; the completion of the Holy Spirit; having both applications of the Holy Spirit, the infilling (**2**) and the enduing upon; the

completion of the New Creation man; hidden in Him (covered on the inside and outside by the Holy Spirit, related to the shadow and type of the Ark of the Covenant **19**); the oil **5548 xríō**

3b Speaking in tongues: the evidence of **3a**; speak with new tongues; with stammering lips and an unknown tongue, He will speak to this people; praying in the Spirit; praying in tongues; speaking mysteries to God; face-to-face (**3a**) conversation; our conversation that is in heaven; prayer language; He who speaks in a tongue edifies himself; praying in tongues while inclining our spiritual ear with an expectation to hear/perceive (**4**) what the Holy Spirit is saying; while praying in tongues we set our affection (**7d**) on things above (**17a**); finely tune into His frequency; tongues makes us "light sensitive" (**10**); pray with the spirit (and pray with the understanding that comes from what we hear in the spirit **4**); pray without ceasing; making melody in our hearts to God; an important component of the two-edged sword that divides between soul and spirit—**3c**; the threshing sledge with sharp teeth (**19**); the winnowing fan (**19**); two-edged mouth (part of the Sword of the Spirit **4a**); He carried me away in the Spirit

3c Baptism by Fire: sanctification; sanctify **37 hagiazó;** set apart; the work of the Spirit; tongues of fire that separate; separated to God; separated from the Adamic nature; burning up anything that's left from the Adamic nature; sanctify them by your Word (**1c**), your Word is truth; continually washed by the water of the Word (**1c**); continually cleansed from all unrighteousness; the God of peace Himself is sanctifying us entirely (spirit, soul and body); unquenchable fire that burns up the dross; dividing tongues as of fire; **1266 diamerizó:** the division (facilitated by **3a**) that separates soul and flesh from spirit; discerns (divides) between thoughts (soul **17**) and intents of the heart (spirit **16**); separate to Me Barnabas and Saul for the work to which I have called them; called and separated for ministry; fasting; to be tried (**7c**) with fire

3d Fruit of the Spirit: the result of the transforming work of the Spirit; spiritual fruit; harvest; virtue; godliness; love; joy; peace **1515 eiréné;** patience **3115 makrothumia;** kindness; gentleness; self-control; produces outward moral behavior; fruitful in every good work; we bear much fruit (when we abide in the vine **2a**); fruit is the result of good works we do being led by the Spirit (**2a**); Spirit-empowered behavior; God-inspired behavior

3e Spiritual gifts: the ministry manifestation of the Spirit (**3**); diversities of gifts; differences of ministries; diversities of activities; word of wisdom; word of knowledge; faith; gifts of healings; working of miracles; prophecy; discerning of spirits; different kinds of tongues and interpretation of tongues only possible through **2a**, **4**, **4a** and **10**); by pursuing love, spiritual gifts follow; love (**1a**) is the power of spiritual gifts

3f Glory: good opinion; praise; honor; **3519 kabowd; 1391 doxa;** an especially divine quality; splendor; give more weight to; worship; rejoice; God has magnified (**1431 gadal**) His Word above His name; believe God and His Word above what we see with our eyes (**7**); **Opposite: 7043 qalal** give no weight; treat lightly; treat with contempt; insignificant; curse

4 Living water: 4487 rhéma Word of the Holy Spirit (always related to the written Word of God **1c**); the living (**1g**) Word (**1c**); rivers of living water; the revealed (**10**) Word (**1c**); hearing/perceiving (**189 akoé**) the voice of the Holy Spirit; causes faith (**7**) to arise; interpretation; the expectation of tongues; the purpose of tongues; our daily bread; manna from heaven; we hear and only do what we hear the Father say (in submitted relationship **2a**); the fountain of life; whoever drinks will never thirst; a fountain of water springing up unto everlasting life (**1g**); His methods of communication; His intrinsically good (**32**) word that originates from Him and is empowered (**3**) by Him; **3708 horaó;** He takes of what is mine (Jesus') and declares it to us; (out of our belly **16**) shall flow rivers of living water; our heavenly conversation; perceiving; His Spirit bears witness with our spirit (**16**)

4a The rhéma Word of God that we speak: the Sword of the Spirit (**3a + 4 = 4a**); the double-mouthed sword **1366 distomos;** speaking out of the Spirit (related to **2a, 4** and **10** because it comes from revelation relationship and hearing); the grace-filled word that we speak; directly related to **13** and **13a** because ministry requires hearing and it edifies the body; the prophetic word; prophecy; prophetic voice; the good word to speak in due season; the word that is grace poured upon our lips; His words that He wants to put in our mouth; "It is written..."; the apples of gold that we should speak in pictures of silver; five smooth stones; speaking to the wind and the waves; say to the mountain be removed and be cast into the sea; I will pray with the spirit (**3b**), and I

will also pray with the understanding (**17a**); I will pray from the understanding received from praying in the spirit

4b Refuse to hear: "they" refuse to hear (who don't accept tongues is how God speaks to His people); "they" who are snared and caught and fall backwards from not studying the Word while praying in tongues in order to hear Him

5 Grace: His unmerited favor; the blessings we don't deserve (relates to His mercy **6**); His willingness to use His ability on our behalf even though we don't deserve it; abundance of grace; standing in grace (favor); blessing and protection; grace and peace be multiplied to you; His covenant loyalty towards us; lovingkindness; we access grace by faith (**7**); we are standing in grace; the lamp (**10**) to our feet shows us we're standing in grace (related to **12**); we come boldly to the throne of grace; under grace, not law (**24**), sin doesn't have dominion over us anymore

5a Grace provisions: His exceedingly great and precious promises; grace provisions (healing, provision, protection, favor); day-to-day salvation (**1e**); the things freely given to us by God (through **1**); our Provider, Jehovah Jireh (**1b**), freely gives us all things; He supplies all our needs according to His riches in glory; we find grace to help in time of need; all things He has freely given us (**1**); all He won for us; the blessings of Deuteronomy 28

6 Mercy: because of the blood; having obtained mercy (we find grace **5** to help); don't get what we deserve (relates to **5**); made acceptable to God by His mercy (relates to justification **8** by faith in Christ **1e**)

7 Faith: faith in Christ, the author and finisher of our faith; justified by faith; related to **1** and **8**; believe in your heart and confess with your mouth (**1b**); believer; speaking from faith (vs confession unto faith **7a**); faith-filled words; faith comes by hearing/spiritually perceiving (**4**); faith that arises; "Amen; let it be to me according to your word..."; the prayer of faith will save the sick; laying on of hands (to release the anointing **3**); shield of faith; above all; boldness and strength that comes from faith; withstand **436 anthistémi;** stand **2476 hístēmi;** take a stand (related to **12**); establish an important principle to govern our life by; feet shod; immovable posture; stand fast; hold our ground based on where we sit; prepared to take a stand; the preparation of the gospel of peace (**1**) = being prepared to stand (feet shod) in faith that we have peace with God (**1**); without faith it's impossible to please Him; we have access by faith into this grace (**5**) in which we stand (**15**); standing in grace, we access it by faith; automatic corresponding actions of faith; the automatic divine response; faith without works is dead; give glory, honor and praise to God by believing Him (**3f**); fully persuaded that God is able to do; trust the Lord; raising our expectations (to receive of our inheritance **1i**); every spirit that confesses Jesus is of God

7a Meditate on the Word day and night: seek revelation (**10**) in fellowship with the Holy Spirit (**2a**); believing unto faith; confession (of the Word **1c**) unto salvation (**1e**); meditate on the Word until faith arises; meditating on the Word until fully persuaded; we believe and confess the Word until true Biblical faith arises and produces automatic corresponding actions of faith (**7**); muse; mutter; relates to **1c** (Scripture) and **3b** (tongues); give attention to my Word, incline your ear (**4**) to my sayings (while praying in tongues **3b**); do not let them depart from your mouth; Bible study; study to show thyself approved; abide in me (**2a**) and let my words abide in you; looking unto Jesus, the author and finisher of our faith (**7**); consider Him and His salvation He provided us (**1**); look to the Lord, the God of our salvation (**1**);

7b Ask and you shall receive: believe you receive when you pray; ask what you desire and it shall be done for you; believe we receive when we pray; ask anything according to my will; praying according to His will; we have the petitions we ask; whatever you ask in my name I will do it; freely receive; putting a faith demand on our inheritance (**1i**); putting a faith demand on our everyday needs (**5a**)

7c The testing of our faith: the perfecting (maturing) work that perfects and completes us, by which we lack nothing; think it not strange concerning the fiery trial which is to try you; the trial of your faith, being much more precious than of gold; to be tried (with fire **3c**)

7d Ask, seek, knock: spiritual appetite; deep thirst; hunger and thirst; purposeful pursuit; **1377 diókó;** diligently seek; **2147 heuriskó;** our relentless inquiry (to seek His wisdom **10**); do not let them (knowledge **1c**, wisdom **10**, understanding **17a**) depart from your eyes; the glory of kings to search out a matter (relates to **10**); if anyone lacks wisdom (**10**) let him ask of God; ask for wisdom not doubting; call unto me and I will answer you; set your affection on things above (in order to receive spiritual understanding **17a**); pursue love, desire spiritual (**13a**)

7e Speak to the mountain; speak life (**1g**); speak to the wind and the waves; take authority (**15**); speaking out of spiritual understanding (**17a**) of our heavenly position in Christ (**15**), as opposed to speaking a rhéma word (**4a**); only speak a word (and my servant will be healed); send the word of faith

7f Take no thought, saying...; speak death (**20**); speak out of natural understanding (**17b**)

8 The righteousness of God: righteousness by faith in Christ; directly related to **1e**; right-standing with God; we've been made the righteousness of God in Christ; the gift of righteousness; breastplate of righteousness; Abrahamic covenant; all the families of the earth blessed along with the believing Abraham; related to **1**, **1e** and **7**; the blessing of Abraham; justification by faith; eternally justified; present yourselves holy and blameless; holiness (by faith in Christ); so that He may establish your hearts blameless in holiness; the ministry of the Spirit; the ministry of righteousness that exceeds much more in glory (than the ministry of condemnation **24**); skilled in the word of righteousness

8a Unskilled in the word of righteousness: immature; babe; partaker of milk; not fully understanding the righteousness of God by faith in Christ (**8**)

9 The New Creation man: we are a new creature; the New Creation heart; the heart that has His law written on it; through it, God causes us to walk (**12**) in His statutes (**3d**); slaves to righteousness; the old man has been crucified with Christ; newness of life (**1g**); created in His image; we have the nature of God (in our spirit **16**); redeemed nature; having been born (**1g**) of incorruptible seed; as He is so are we in this world; partakers of the divine nature; the believer; we are His sheep (and we do hear **4** His voice); we are spiritual creatures (**16**), having been born again (**1g**)

10 Revelation light: the light that gives life (**1g**) to men; revelation; **5461 phótizó;** flash of revelation understanding (facilitated by praying in tongues **3b**); on this rock I will build my church; the rock of revelation; through revelation He opens the eyes of our spiritual understanding (**17a**); wisdom which leads to spiritual understanding (**17a**); if any man lacks wisdom, let him ask of God; every good gift from above; wisdom that is from above; open eyes; unveiled; eyes that see and ears that hear; (directly related to

2a, **4** and **17a**); what is revealed; revealing the mysteries of God; to you it has been given to know the mystery of the kingdom of God; attaining to all riches of the full assurance of understanding, to the knowledge of the mystery of God; in whom are hidden all the treasures of wisdom and knowledge; wisdom **1219 batsar;** practical wisdom **5428 phronésis;** to know the things that have been freely given to us by God (**1**); (by the anointing **2a**) we know all things; knowing the deep things of God; His supernatural insight; He shows us (through **2a**) great and mighty things which we do not know; comparing spiritual things with spiritual; recognizing the Messiah; that you may be able to comprehend; the result of interpretation of tongues (**3e**); revelations are the bricks that build us up (**13a**) on our most holy faith (**7**)

10a Children of the light: offspring of revelation (because of **2**); directly connected to **17a**; ...and we know all things...

10b Lack of knowledge: My people perish for lack of knowledge (directly connected to **17b**); ignorance; different to darkness of the unredeemed (**20**) since the redeemed have the ability to know God through **2**, whereas the unredeemed can't know God; for we do not know what we should pray (until we pray in tongues **3b** which facilitates **4**); the uninformed

10c Natural knowledge: knowledge of the Word without revelation; knowledge without the breath of the Spirit; academics; religion; void of God's wisdom; persuasive words of human wisdom (related to **27**); excellence of speech; the wisdom of this age; the wisdom of men; (relates to **27** and **17b**); puffed up in knowledge

11 Spiritual warfare: submitting to God (to God's truth **1**) and resisting the devil (his lies **21**); actively take up the whole armor; submitting to the renewing of the mind (**17a**); guarding the seed of the Word (from the birds of prey); enforce our victory in Christ (**1**); casting down arguments **2507 kathaireó;** taking captive every argument (**21**) that tries to rise above our knowledge of **1**; the full armor of God; the weapons of our warfare; defensive and offensive weaponry; **3833 panoplia;** helmet of salvation (**1f**); to practically exercise saved thinking (**1f 4993 sóphroneó**); gird our waist with truth (**1c**); gird up the loins (**3751 osphus**) of the mind; reproductive ability of the renewed mind (salvation thinking **1f**); using sound, healthy (**5198 hugiainó**) doctrine (**1c**) to stand

in faith (**7**); sober **3525 néphó;** free from illusion/intoxicating influences

12 Walk: conduct our life; regulate our life; govern our life; **4043 peripateó;** perspective to live life by; His Word (**1c**) is a lamp (**10**) to our feet (which shows us we are standing in grace **5**) and a light (**10**) unto our path (which way to walk); the revelation light (**10**) illuminating our path shows us which way to walk; walking is related to where we stand in grace **5** and our stand of faith **7**; walk in the Spirit (**2a**) and we won't fulfill the lust of the flesh (**18**); wisdom (**10**) meets us at intersecting paths where decisions must be made and paths (to walk) must be chosen; practically living

13 The ministry: the word of reconciliation (relates to **1**); the equipping of the saints for the work of the ministry; the five-fold ministry is given to some, not all (apostle, prophet, evangelist, pastor and teacher); **4462 rhabbouni;** preaching the gospel (relates to **4** because true ministry comes out of the hearing); expounding of the Scriptures; preaching the gospel under the power of the Spirit; witnessing to others; sower of the seed; boldly walking and speaking; standing up; raised voice; preaching Christ teaching; preaching; ministry of healing; (related to **3** because it's Spirit-empowered); ambassadors for Christ; God's purpose; the called according to His purpose; separated (**3c**) to His purpose; His calling; bearing with one another in love

13a Edification: edification, exhortation and comfort to men; edification of the church; **3618 oikodomeó;** let it be for the edification of the church you seek to excel; pursue (**1377 diókó**) love, desire spiritual gifts; built securely on the rock (of revelation **10**) relates to **1f** because it leads to healthy salvation thinking; building your house upon the rock (of revelation **10**); through wisdom (**10**) a house is built; by understanding (**17a**) it is established; by knowledge (**10**) the rooms are filled; the grace-filled word we speak (**4a**) edifies the hearer; unbelievers are convinced and convicted by tongues with interpretation and prophecy; tongues are for a sign to the unbeliever

14 The Resurrection: He presented Himself alive after suffering; speaking; teaching; walking with them for 40 days; our future resurrection

15 Authority: delegated authority in Christ; **1849 exhousia;** authorized; He raised us up and made us sit together with Christ; seated at the right hand of the Father; our heavenly position in Christ; the devil (**21a**) is under our feet; we are standing in grace (**5**); dominion; joint heirs (**1i**) with Christ; in His name; (those who are led by the Holy Spirit **2a** are) authorized and empowered (**3**) sons of God; keys of the kingdom; binding and loosing; sent the same way Jesus was sent (to only do and say **4a** what He heard **4** the Father say)

16 Spirit: our spirit; the inner man; **2836 koilia;** spiritual being; incorruptible spirit-man (relates to **2** and **9**) developing our spiritual senses; learned spiritual skills; (His Spirit bears witness **2a** with) our spirit; out of our belly (shall flow rivers of living water **4**)

16a Spirit realm: heavenlies; heavenly places; spiritual realm; **4152 pneumatikos; 4151 pneúma; 2032 epouranios;** invisible realm

17 Soul: mind, will and emotions; thought life; intellectual mind; **5590 psuché** decision-maker; free will; the seat of conscious thought, feelings and reasoning

17a Spiritual understanding: living spiritually minded (requires **1c** and **2a**, and results in **10**); our soul in the ongoing process of redemption by the renewing of the mind; be renewed in the spirit of your mind; spiritual perception; spiritual reasoning (with the Holy Spirit **2a**); that the man of God may be complete (thoroughly equipped for every good **32** work **2a**); spiritually discerned; come and reason with me (says God); bless the Lord o my soul, forget not (remember) all His benefits (in other words, consider the situation according to what He has done vs what we see in the natural); remember Him; but we have the mind of Christ; God's perspective; Christian maturity; divine viewpoint; God's perspective

17b Natural understanding: carnally minded; leaning to our own understanding (causes **18a**); opposite of **17a** and **10**; do not walk (**12**) as the Gentiles walk, in the emptiness of natural reasoning, being alienated from the life of God (while saved); the futility of the mind; reasoning according to the five-sense realm; unregenerate thinking (residual thinking from the Adamic nature; spiritually blind/darkness of understanding (even though redeemed); what natural ear can't hear and eye can't see; walking (**12**) by sight, looking at natural circumstances; the natural man (even though redeemed) results in **10b**; the natural man cannot receive the things of the Spirit of God, for they are foolishness unto him, neither can he know

them because they are spiritually discerned; separated from intimacy with God (**3a**), even being saved, through relying on the natural intellect (**10c**) and self-effort (**18a**); existing in a withered state, being cut off from the life of God; the cares of the world that choke the Word (**1c**); thorns and thistles; unfruitfulness; opposite of **1f**; corrupt (natural) words we speak from natural understanding; Spirit-to-soul relationship

17c Sin consciousness: looking at our failures; evil conscience of unbelief; judgment of ourselves according to the good and evil mindset

18 Body and flesh: not yet redeemed; still has corruption at work in it; corrupted flesh; another law working in our members (**20**); Adam was born physically eternal but fell (**23**) to physically temporal; we are born into a body that is physically dying; the outer man; this earthen vessel; our members; body of sin; the lust of the flesh; the voice of the flesh; we all once conducted ourselves in the lusts of the flesh; the underlying urge of the flesh; the strong desire of the flesh; born of the flesh; natural man; the outward man that is perishing; children in understanding

18a Leaning on the arm of the flesh: walking according to the flesh; self effort; making flesh our strength; opposite of puting no confidence in the flesh (**1d**); I can of Myself do nothing; the flesh profits nothing; under the curse of the law (**24**); seeking to keep the law in our own strength; attempting to be justified by the law (**24**); becoming entangled again with a yoke of bondage; yoked to the law; seeking to establish our own righteousness; becoming circumcised (symbolistic of coming back under the Old Covenant); debtor to keep the whole law; subject to corruption; frustrate the grace of God; make Christ of no effect; estranged from Christ; Christ will profit you nothing; fallen from grace; leading ourselves by ourselves; sowing to the flesh; self-willed; they covered themselves; they hid themselves; the tendency to live self-willed because they're separated from God; self-willed propensity; dead works (vs good works **2a**) that will be burned up in the end (**25**); chaff; the Ishmael effect

18b Eternal flesh: will be fully redeemed and transformed at the resurrection; future redeemed flesh

19 Shadows and types: ordinances of the temple; feasts of Israel; prophecies of Jesus in the Old Covenant; Jesus is the substance;

the picture is the shadow and type, the real thing is the substance; Communion; breaking of bread; ordinances of the New Covenant— Baptism and Communion; the winnowing fan; the threshing floor; the threshing sledge

20 The death that spread to all men: the corrupted sin nature; the curse; the cursed earth and flesh; the pronouncement of the curse; the bondage of corruption condemnation unto death; dead in trespasses and sin; spiritually separated from God; dead **3498 nekros;** enmity with God; without God; children of wrath; cut off/severed from the vine; alienated from the life of God; the captives; sinners; children of wrath; born into death; two deaths (**4191 muth**); the penalty of sin; unredeemed; the corruption that is in the earth and flesh; the world (individuals) who cannot receive the Spirit of truth; the world (individuals) under the sway of the wicked one; the fallen world (**27**); **1311 diaphtheiró;** the old man; the good and evil mindset; the blind; eyes that don't see and ears that don't hear; veiled eyes; spiritual darkness; darkness of understanding; naked (no clothing of glory); dust-to-dust; slow physical death (**18**); sweat; hard toil

20a Sin: the works of the flesh; another law working in our members; iniquity; adultery, fornication, uncleanness, lewdness, idolatry, sorcery, hatred, contentions, jealousies, outbursts of wrath, selfish ambitions, dissensions, heresies, envy, murders, drunkenness, revelries, and the like

21 The devil's arguments: subtle; cunning temptations to doubt God's Word and believe the devil's lies instead; arguments that rise up; vain imaginations; the warfare (**11**) that we need spiritual weapons for; the devil's sifting; the devil's wiles; strategies; tactics; tricks; strongholds; attempts to control our thinking; master of illusion; scheming; predictable preset methods (**3180 methodeia**); searching inquiries; organized evil-doing; craftiness; fear; deception; devices/designs; accusations; the accuser of the brethren; condemnation; accusation according to the good and evil mindset; feeling naked and ashamed (having no clothing of glory, being separated from God); illusion; intoxicating influences; tempting us to look at natural circumstances (**17b**); the temptation to walk by sight (**17b**); usurp; attack of the enemy; fiery darts; the evil day; smite the loins; deal a fatal blow to the reproductive ability of the loins or renewed mind in Christ (relates to **1f**, **11** and **17a**); voice of condemnation; you may well put up with it (deception); doctrines of demons; their message that spreads like cancer; profane and idle babblings; hearing and accepting wrong thinking (**17b**)

21a The devil: deceiving spirits; false spirits; demonic; the serpent; the enemy; the wicked one; familiar spirits; demonic presence; birds of prey (that come immediately to steal **21** the seed of the Word **1c**); fowls of the air; the prince of the power of the air, the spirit who now works in the sons of disobedience; do not believe every spirit; test the spirits; false prophets; other gods; false christs; a different spirit; a different gospel; false relationship with deceiving spirits; false signs and wonders; great signs and wonders to deceive even the elect; perilous times; the counterfeit of the enemy; mystical practices; **2888 kosmokratór;** the ruler of this world; spiritual hosts of wickedness; the kingdom of darkness

22 Face-to-face: against; towards; **4314 pros;** face-to-face with God; face-to-face against the enemy

23 Adam's disobedience: the fall of man; through one man sin entered the world; one man's disobedience; unbelief; evil heart of unbelief; doubting God's Word (the strategy of the devil **21**); leads to **18a**

24 The law: the law of sin and death; the handwriting of requirements written against us; the ten commandments; the ministry of death; the ministry of condemnation; the bondage of the law; the law that causes sin to abound; the yoke of the law; the yoke of bondage; the letter that kills

25 The Day: the judgment; the fire that tests and reveals each man's work (good works from being led by the Spirit **2a** or dead works from self-effort **18a**); the end of the age

26 The kingdom of God: governmental position we submit to; anywhere the King reigns; they preached the kingdom of God; kingdom life is where the King rules; everything that aligns with His purpose; plan and pursuit of God

26a The kingdom of heaven: heaven on earth; open heaven; windows of heaven open to us; on earth as it is in heaven; the kingdom of God is within you; (relates to **2** because we are the temple); we call heaven to earth; every spiritual blessing in the heavenlies; every good gift (**10**) come down from above

26b Kingdom principles: sowing and reaping: spiritual principles

27 World: 2889 kosmos; universe; world order; inhabitants of the world; the collective unredeemed (**20**); we once walked according to the course of this world; the rulers of this age; don't be conformed to this world (age **28**) that lives according to the good and evil mindset/paradigm; those who go down to Egypt for help, and rely on horses, who trust in chariots; the spirit of the world; the system of the unrighteous mammon

28 Age: world; eon **165 aión;** a cycle of time; this present age; the fallen age; the church age; the age of rest; the millennial age; the age of innocence

29 In this manner: thus; in this way; **3779 houtó**

30 So that: 2443 hina; in order that

31 Sure expectation: hope **1680 elpis;** better translated as sure expectation; earnest expectation

32 Good: 18 agathos; intrinsically good, good in nature, good whether it be seen to be so or not; God's intrinsically good nature

32a Good: 2570 kalos; beautiful, good, outward appearance of good; as an outward sign of the inward good, noble, honorable character

33 Far surpassing: 5236 huperbolé; superlatively beyond measure; exceedingly far beyond; throwing beyond

34 As of: like, as if, **5616 hósei**